Money,
Emotions,
and the
Recovery Process

by Mary Raphel, L.C.S.W.

To order copies of this book, write
to:
Enrichment Resources
7402 York Road, Suite 300
Baltimore, MD 21204

*Dedicated with love and gratitude
to my family, friends and
recovering DA members everywhere.*

Money, Emotions, and the Recovery Process

Table of Contents

AUTHOR'S NOTES

Throughout this book, you will see references to a "Higher Power." A Higher Power can be anything you want it to be. It can refer to the Universe, Spirit, God, Nature, a Higher Self, etc. The significance of a Higher Power is that we acknowledge that there is something more powerful than us that has a plan of which we are intended to be a part. While the Higher Power is not human and therefore has no sex or gender, it may be referred to as "he" simply for the sake of ease in writing. Hopefully, no one will need to take offense as it is not intended to have any added meaning.

Although this book is copyrighted, anyone is free to duplicate any portion of it and freely use it for the purposes of 12 Step Recovery.

Acknowledgements

I want to thank my Higher Power for putting incredible and fabulous people in my life when I needed them. I am especially grateful to Baltimore DA for encouraging me and believing I could complete this book and never letting me give up even when I wanted to. I also feel indebted to my clients for sharing their stories with me and showing me again and again that all of this really does work.

A very special thanks to Ann Smith who has always remained excited for me and supportive in my sharing what I know. I also want to acknowledge Nancy Michaelson who in the early days helped me to clarify so much of the material presented here. I remain grateful to both her and Jim Bomgardner for venturing out with me to take the book material on the road. The miles we traveled hold many fond memories. Thanks too, to Rita Dilworth and her colleagues for showing up to bring all of this together. Rita's serenity and patience are incredible gifts and a source of inspiration to me.

Most of all there probably aren't enough words or hugs to thank my daughter Melissa and Jessica Shifflett, my secretary. Without their uncomplaining diligence and willingness to work under pressure none of this would be in print today. Their flexibility, tolerance of change and overall enthusiasm about the material kept me sane. Their saving me from my dreaded computer taught each of us a lot. Lastly, I want to acknowledge from a special place in my heart the people of the Baltic Countries in Lithuania, Latvia and Estonia for reminding me of where we came from in relation to lack and for showing a group of us as professionals visiting there that there is still so much more to do. As Americans, we are truly blessed to be among the most prosperous people in the world. Thank you God.

Introduction

Twelve Step recovery programs have led many of us to greater health and hope. Yet, after two or so years of recovery I often hear people ask "where do I go from here?". Life feels better but not happy. There is much more to be grateful for but joy remains elusive. New jobs have been acquired. Self respect has increased. Things begin to feel comfortable for perhaps the first time in many years. For some reason, though, it is not enough. There is still that hole inside that just isn't satisfied. In spite of everything, we still feel empty and deprived.

Without a doubt, I grew up thinking "more is better." It didn't matter more what; whether it is love, money, sex, time, food, clothes, etc. having more was supposed to be better. In operating out of this belief, I have always felt deprived. I have never had enough. As a result, at one point in my life this led me to juggling a full time job, three part time jobs, and a lot of debt.

In my professional work as a therapist, I realized that I am not alone in this scarcity thinking. I have watched others experience great pain operating out of the same resounding message. Particularly for the addicted person, whatever the substance, the feeling of deprivation has led many to self destruction.

In recovery physical change happens relatively quickly, often within the first year. Emotional recovery begins to follow.

However, spiritual recovery cannot happen without an examination of one's attitude, a shift in thinking from scarcity and aloneness to abundance and a benevolent "Higher Power" as the provider and source of all good irregardless of outside circumstances. For over twenty years, I have believed that one of my assignments in life is to write a book. In delaying this, all I knew was that whatever I would write needed to provide some tools, a source of hope and a strong feeling of inspiration for others who have struggled like myself and are willing to do anything to let that go. My family, my friends, my co-workers, and my clients have all served as my inspiration. It is with inspiration and a lot of courage that I have seen miracles happen. Hopefully with this book, we can all go from wanting to having everything that we are entitled to receive. For what I have discovered is that in truth there is no scarcity, only a blocking of abundance, and a belief we don't deserve.

God Grant You
Days of Brilliance

By Enid Gittens Foreman

God grant you days of brilliance,
May increasing joy fill your heart,
God's gift of love, your daily experience,
From the moment your brilliant day starts.
God grant you days that are marvelous,
Endowed with divine happiness, supreme,
Days triumphantly victorious,
Beyond your most treasured dreams!

PART I

1 *A Victim says*
   "What has the world done to me?
   A Master says
   "What is it I have created?"
                  — *Carl Thomas*

Deprivation

Tracey was forced to leave her violent, alcoholic home at age 16. She is a recovering alcoholic and drug addict, involved in a 12 Step Program for over 5 years. Tracey is a second year nursing student and terrified of getting her own apartment. She presently lives in an abusive, hostage type relationship serving a 70 year old woman as a companion. Tracey errands for the woman in exchange for room and board. There is no way for Tracey to ever please her boss/landlady, yet she endlessly tries. Frustrated at never having done enough, Tracey lashes out in anger. She then feels so guilty that she feverishly tries to make it up with greater efforts and giving even more of her time to this woman's demands. The cycle of employer/landlady abuse only becomes fueled by Tracey's own self abuse, and the pattern continues. Why does she stay?

Jim is a recovering alcoholic of over 3 years, doing well in maintaining his sobriety. At a recent AA function, Jim was responsible for a raffle, and in drawing the winning name picked his own. Immediately, he put it back without saying anything to anyone. What was wrong with Jim claiming the prize?

Ann grew up in a house having no bedroom of her own. She had to sleep in the frequently wet basement on a mattress on the floor. She often experienced bugs crawling all over her. At the age of 7, she was forced to go with a male neighbor who sexually abused her regularly over a 5 year period of time. When pleading with her mother for permission to not go, her mother insisted. The neighbor was providing gifts and giving her mother money for the episodes of abusing her daughter and her mother was not about to lose this income. As an adult, Ann married and bought a home which later proved to be infested with bugs. The house had been built on a nest of insects which could not be exterminated. Once again, she spent years awakening to bugs crawling on and around her. Is this a coincidence?

Growing up Fran was told that the secret of success was to get an education and work hard. Only after numerous firings, has she been able to admit that she hates being an accountant and that her workaholism is killing her. Filled with anger and rage, Fran has great difficulty letting go of the perfectionism that keeps her from having anything she truly wants. What has led her to become so "anorexic" in the area of dreams and self care?

All of these individuals are recovering in 12 Step Programs based on the principles of AA (Alcoholics Anonymous). They have worked long and hard and have all met with some new level of improved functioning and comfortability. Yet, in spite of the increased manageability of their lives, there is something missing. Life is better, but not the "happy, joyous, and free" as each 12 Step Program promises. In both my personal and professional experience, what I see is that we live lives of quiet deprivation. Having grown up in dysfunctional families, many of us have learned to be victims. We have become passive, subservient, dependent, fearful, and resigned. The deprivation has taken many forms. For some it is deprivation of very basic needs: money, food, clothes, shelter, and space. For others the deprivation refers to a lack of information, identity, time, emotional support, and love.

Contributing to the limitations we often find in the home, society promotes the idea that we had better hurry; time is running out. We become an easy mark for salesmen as they say "this is your last chance to get a really good deal." We are led to believe there will never be such an opportunity again. News reports are filled with scarcity messages: prices going up; a rise in unemployment; save before its too late; and of course the horror and reminder of our national debt.

Our national debt is now over four trillion dollars. Perhaps we should take a moment and try to visualize exactly how much money that is. Suppose you had a job pay at $1.00 per second, working day and night, at $86,400 per day. It would take 31.7 years to earn only a billion dollars. That is not even close to what you would begin to need to erase the debt that we as a nation have incurred.

More and more we hear of businesses and individuals filing for bankruptcies. These too, are now at a record high. On a more personal level, just where is it that our money goes? According to the records of the Tax Foundation Estimates, the average American works each year:

16 weeks to pay taxes

10 weeks for housing

7 weeks for food

3 weeks for clothing

3 weeks for transportation

3 weeks for medical care

2 weeks for recreation

6 weeks for everything else

The feeling of deprivation pervades all aspects of one's life. It can be felt in every area: finances, relationships, health, and happiness. It permeates all decisions and the outcome of those decisions. It goes to the depths of one's soul. It feels like a gaping wound exists, a hole that seems bottomless and insatiable. Whatever we get feels like too little, too late. The fact that there are no clear pleasant memories of the good in the past make the feelings of deprivation even more pronounced. At this point some settle, stagnate, and give up having any dreams. No belief in possibility remains or the belief relies upon some kind of magic happening to make things better. For the rest of us, we know no one person will ever be able to fill the void. It scares us to realize how deep and empty our well is. Shame pervades our thoughts. Our feelings become "bad" and our neediness must be hidden. We put on a mask of independence, not needing anything or anyone. We take pride in how little we can get by on. However, getting a few crumbs reminds us of our starvation. The crumbs are never enough. Our obsession becomes focused on how we can get more. We lose any sense of what life is really about. We can't be spiritual. Something else, that which we have been deprived of becomes our new God. We have fallen into a hole. In the darkness, we have no idea how to get out. The darkness becomes all encompassing. The unanswered question remains "What about me?"

With Tracey, what we find is a past full of fear for her safety and a lack of any kind of security. As a result, she repeatedly forces herself to stick with draining situations and circumstances, grateful for any "crumbs" she may get. While trying to develop and maintain an attitude of "I don't expect..." and rationalizing "I really don't want..." she actually prevents any good from coming to her. She feels forced to lean on others, expects of them, and later blames them or herself when things don't work out. Magnetically, she is drawn to what she knows and continuously attracts people who will disappoint her. As time goes on, she begins to resent the wealth of others, while at the same time depriving herself. Tracey, as those of us like her, becomes a victim dwelling on troubles, disease, war and suffering in the world. We become part of the negativity and disease, as opposed to becoming part of the solution and cure. Our growing bitterness and criticism of other's helps to keep us stuck. We become possessive, fearing additional loss. Blaming ourselves for our lack, we continuously pull ourselves down by replaying anything we perceive as a mistake within our minds. We let any hurdle, obstacle or problem stop us. At the same time we become full of hostility, inferiority, envy, hatred, and jealousy. Everything becomes complicated and ongoing crises prevails. Opportunities for change are met with both resistance and fear.

Jim has learned to cheat himself. For Jim, it is OK to have only what is needed. He gave up having "wants" long ago when he was still a child. Any deep longings must be kept hidden. With such strong feelings of unworthiness, he worries about taking more than his share in life. He has worked hard to convince himself that this is as good as it gets. Much of Jim's time, as with Tracey, is spent dwelling upon a belief in lack and limitation even though we obviously live in a world of abundance. On what he considers a good day, Jim believes there is virtue in being poor. Having material things is not spiritual. He considers himself selfish, should any desire surface. It is not OK for Jim to ask for any increased good and he feels terribly guilt ridden if he receives any prosperity. Jim expects to have to struggle and can be found dragging himself through life. He is known to suffer from what we call "compulsive mediocrity" in that he will only go so far and then pull back. After pulling back, he may drift and in doing so become a victim of the vicious circle of financial uncertainty and strain. For many of us, we find ourselves living on the edge, believing in lack, even when we may be in the midst of abundance, and block any good from coming to us. As we feel sorry for ourselves, our false humility prevents us from growing and having. The deprivation cycle sneaks in with the "someday syndrome." An unusual amount of time and thought is given to daydreaming and fantasizing about wealth and success. Before long, money is increasingly on our minds. Arguments with spouses and children over money surface. To cheer ourselves, we begin spending. Feeling guilt ridden, we get behind on payments and obsess about overdue bills. The search for a quick fix begins. The lottery, consolidation loans, get rich quick schemes, and bankruptcy all surface as solutions. This inevitably leads us back to "someday" and the fantasy about having what we really don't believe we deserve.

Ann grew up in a world that taught her fear, anxiety, and worry. As for many of us, daily feelings of loss, isolation, shame, and anger can become overwhelming. We focus on our inadequacies, past mistakes, failures, and become immobilized by dwelling on the past and dreading the future. When the deprivation has involved severe physical as well as emotional neglect, there is often self depreciation, embarrassment, and a strong sense of unworthiness. Ann learned to be patient and do without while being over responsible in giving to others. Her deprivation became an accumulation of unmet wants and needs bringing along with it feelings of being bad and a failure. To cover over the pain of the past, it is not uncommon to get involved in a hundred different tasks. Energies become very scattered, caretaking and dealing with constant crisis. Through enabling others, Ann contributes to and creates her own deprivation. Without any awareness, we can create limitations and accept and live with them as though they were real. A poverty stricken person is always imagining lack and limitation. Checks bouncing, business failure, and foreclosures become dreaded fears. Studies show that the poor are so caught up in their present problems that they do not know how to constructively plan or think ahead. Their time and energies are spent struggling and battling present crisis and fears.

There appears to be among victims of deprivation a tendency to hold onto worry and fears.

Many do not want to give them up. As professional worriers, we have the ability to picture some undesirable situation not vaguely, but vividly. We play this mental picture over and over catastrophizing as we go along. Each time we horriblize it even more. After visualizing the scene in such a manner, we find ourselves surprised that we feel anxious and often can't eat or sleep. It never occurs to us to picture a desirable end result and see that in detail. Such a visualization appears to be unthought of and an impossibility. We have become so accustomed to expecting that the worst we approach all of life, even the happiest occasions, with feelings of dread and impending doom. We forget that the more attention we give something by worrying about it, the more we are affirming it and actually bring what we have been dreading right into our lives. We are so good at this that we even worry about why we may not be worried.

Physiologically, we are not created to withstand the chemical reactions of prolonged periods of fear and anxiety. As we think negative, self critical and abusive thoughts, chemical poisons are released in and throughout our bodies. Health deteriorates. We create and compound another area of deprivation. The overall functioning of the organs of our body become negatively affected. Aches and pains become the result of anxious, fear filled thinking. Colitis, ulcers, arthritis, and migraines are just a beginning of how the body responds to what we think.

It is not surprising that Ann was diagnosed with most of these. For while we can rationalize and explain why we have been so deprived of attention, money, love, joy, etc. However, the rationalizations begin to wear thin. We can no longer live in a world of make believe. To ease the pain, we minimize the needs. Along with others, we begin to convince ourselves that we aren't important. With some recovery, however, we know this isn't true. Knowing it increases the pain even more. The neediness grows. The pain of feeling insatiable becomes so consuming that it only feels safe to isolate for fear that someone may see us in all our rawness. The more we are deprived the hungrier we get. We begin to go to any lengths to fill up and live with a fear that maybe there won't be enough. Hoarding, stockpiling, and "anorexic" money starvation sets in. Rolls of toilet paper, cans of tuna, pennies in a jar, more clothes than we ever wear fill our cabinets and closets. Always keeping a spare on hand forces us to load shopping carts beyond reasonable need. The idea of one spare becomes 5 or 6 items stocked on hand. Thinking in terms of what we lack, or may lack, becomes our everyday state of mind. Our thoughts of what we might need becomes the breeding ground for debt. We ferociously set about to "stretch every dollar" and will only shop for what we need if it is on sale.

Fran also finds herself saving for that rainy day. She operates out of an ongoing fear of emergencies and rarely finds herself surprised when they in fact do happen. Added to her fear is the belief, "if I spend what money I have, it will be gone forever and probably be impossible to replace." She treats her money like a buried treasure. Fran views herself and her efforts as the only source for generating income. She believes that hard work alone will bring riches and rewards. Her answer is to expend great physical energy. Fran lives by a "hard work consciousness" and has learned this lesson well. She expects to work hard and struggle. Fran also rejects any idea that work could bring pleasure. Fun at one's job is a foreign concept. It is no wonder that under these circumstances, self pity develops. A great hostility and envy grows towards those who are successful. Persons in positions of authority are resented and defied. Power and control become the dominant issues. Force and self will are used to get what is wanted and ultimately always results in being fired or failure. Before long, we become filled with cynicism, misery, and despair. A highly depressed state of mind evolves. Though the failures appear to be unexplainable, they become personalized within a very short time. Angry, isolated, full of fear and inadequacy, the thinking becomes poisoned. Before long, these negative emotions themselves bring on greater and greater loss in income. Success becomes resented rather than any work being done in positive ways to achieve it. Those of us like Fran always see ourselves at a disadvantage. With a belief in competition, we see ourselves as losers convinced that the wealth in the world will always belong to someone else. What is left is an overserious, exhausted, and strained state of mind that repels prosperity. Joy, laughter, happiness, and peace appear to be totally outside the grasp of a workaholic in deprivation. Having originally turned to work as a way of achieving prosperity, we allow our self will, negative thinking, perfectionism, and need for control to block us from the very things we've wanted. A whirlpool of negative thinking exists. We look for and see the worst in everything. We become rigid and inflexible and try to blame our state of mind on others. It becomes much easier to give up instead of asking anyone for help. We become content to lie in self pity adopting the belief that life is just to difficult for us. Suicide looks like the only way out. No good could possibly lie ahead. The thought of taking any action on our own behalf is dismissed. It all feels hopeless as we become certain of defeat and anticipate that more failure is all that we can expect.

A deprived person is always imagining lack and limitation of all kinds. Living in darkness, filled with anger, resentment, and fear allows us to blame the government, competition, taxes, world conditions, all kinds of people and things outside ourselves. Yet, we have a choice. We have a choice of failure or success. Many of us choose and expect failure. As victims of deprivation, what we suffer from is not a lack of abundance, but a lack of awareness and consciousness. Facts are facts, but our attitudes are a matter of choice. We can choose how we want to react to any given circumstance:

1. with a need to simply run away
2. with resentment, anger, and envy
3. or with courage, wisdom, and support

All of us in recovery at some point in time, have tried the running way. Eventually not getting what we wanted from people, we started trying to get it from inanimate objects. Lack, however, is a state of mind. Many of us in our victim state would like to readily challenge and argue this. Yet, lack can only be remedied when the mind is altered. What goes on in our minds is reflected in all areas of our lives. If we want to change our lives, we need to change our thinking. We can control what goes on in our minds. We can stop intrusive, negative, unhealthy thoughts. It's a choice we can make. Joseph Murphy, author of Your Infinite Power to Be Rich, states that "our words are more powerful than atomic or nuclear energy." The only thing holding us back, keeping us in a state of deprivation is our thinking. We will become poor no matter how much we presently have if we think scarcity and poverty thoughts. We cannot afford the luxury of a negative thought. It only takes us a matter of seconds for our minds to pronounce a death sentence on every inspiration and good idea we have. We look for problems. As Rudyard Kipling states, "words are the most powerful drug used by mankind." Our state of deprivation becomes equally proportional to our negative think-ing. Scarcity thinking creates scarcity. Notice what happens when a snow storm, oil shortage, or gasoline crunch is predicted. There is panic and fear creating scarcity all within itself. Deprivation thinking inevitably leads us to:

- Taking as much as we can for the sake of getting something
- Letting others direct our lives to get crumbs
- Falling apart so someone will take care of us
- Letting others define our reality
- Expecting others to anticipate our needs
- Self abuse and victimization sexually and physically
- Compulsive hoarding and stockpiling - "more is better"
- Falling in love with anyone who shows us any
    kindness at all
- Pushing others away with our neediness
- Letting others take whatever they want from us (because we
    don't deserve)
- Refusing gifts and generosity out of shame and
- Acting on impulse.

There is a way out. Changing our thinking from deprivation and fear to abundance and faith is a path we can pursue. However, before moving on, I want to mention a few additional terms associated with a particular 12 Step Program that, for the purpose of this book, needs to be addressed.

From time to time throughout the course of this book, there will be mention of DA (Debtors Anonymous) and some of that program's tools. DA is a 12 Step Program whose primary purpose is to help others stay solvent and stop incurring debt. Through my experience with this program, I have found that it is really about gaining a clear sense of one's self worth. While being an incredibly helpful program, it appears that few people are aware of its existence. A listing of DA meetings and locations can be found in the appendix of this book. I highly recommend attending DA meetings as a source of support in recovering from the life-style of deprivation.

While not considered by DA to be "approved" literature, Jerrold Mundis does and excellent job in his book How To Get Out of Debt, Stay Out of Debt and Live Prosperously describing the basics concepts of this 12 Step Program.

In DA, attention is given to refraining from incurring any "unsecured debt." Unsecured debt is any debt that is not backed up by some form of collateral such as a car, house, etc. Charging clothes or buying new CD's for your stereo on a credit card are not secured debts. There is no collateral and they can not be repossessed should you negate your payment responsibility. With this in mind, borrowing can only be done when collateral has been offered. If I choose to borrow $500.00 from my brother, for example, I would need to leave him something of mine of equal value perhaps a camera or TV. In DA, after keeping records of expenses and income for a period of time a "Pressure Group Meeting" is held for the purpose of alleviating (not increasing) any pressure a person may be experiencing. This pressure could come from being financially overwhelmed by debts or feeling uncertain about changing jobs or spending a recent windfall that has come our way. A Pressure Group is made up of ourselves and two other persons (preferably a male and a female for both perspectives) who have been abstinent from incurring any new unsecured debt of their own for at least three months and have some experience in the program. What comes out of a Pressure Group Meeting is a "spending plan." This differs from a budget. A budget is a lot like a diet and everyone who has ever been on one of those knows what happens. With a budget (and a diet) we increase our deprivation by restricting ourselves. Ultimately, we react to the deprivation with a binge or a compulsive spending spree leaving us with a feeling of being totally out of control and setting up the vicious debting cycle all over again. With a spending plan we set up categories of both our wants and needs, deciding how much money we want to allot to each category. For example, we may have a food category and a recreation category. We may decide, with pressure group help, to allot $150.00 a month for food and $50.00 a month for recreation. After deciding on the spending plan amounts, we then strive to stay within the planned amounts throughout that month. Our spending plan becomes a statement of our own personal values. There is no imposition of someone else dictating what we should or shouldn't be spending. There is no fear of someone else controlling us or our money. We feel and develop a real clear sense of self responsibility, deciding on our priorities within the resources available to us. Whatever we individually feel is important is important. Most people are very surprised at what comes out of a pressure meeting. After years of feeling lost, fearful and struggling, we find ourselves back on our true path. Forgotten dreams and abandoned hopes return to the surface. With a list of actions to take, a new sense of direction appears to be found.

Having been involved in and working a number of 12 Step Programs myself, I was surprised at how quickly the DA results began to appear. Unlike other 12 Step Programs, in DA the material results and physical recovery becomes tangible, visible, and often readily acquired. With support of the DA Program and use of other information presented in this book, prosperity and abundance can be yours. However, before that can happen we need to look at where some of our limiting messages began. After all, what you think is really what you get.

2 *"Henceforth I ask not good fortune I myself am good fortune."*
—*Walt Whitman*

Family Dynamics

When we look at our families, whether they are alcoholic or simply dysfunctional, what we often find is a parent, who lives in constant financial fear. This parent lives out of the messages "more is better" and "hard work will get you what you need." As a result, this parent may become a workaholic. He or she is always over responsible and may volunteer a significant amount of time serving on all kinds of boards and committees. This parent believes they "owe" others everything and deserve very little for themselves. He or she becomes a prime enabler and is constantly financially rescuing everyone at their own expense.

The other parent is just the opposite. This parent is a compulsive spender. He or she believes and expects that they will be taken care of by their spouse and others. When not getting what he or she thinks is owed to them, they nag, complain, shame and manipulate. While the workaholic parent may be exhausted and suffering from all kinds of stress related illnesses, the other parent spends carefree days planning the next spree or "needed" purchase.

These confusing messages are what get handed down to their children. Much has already been written about the roles children play growing up in addicted and dysfunctional families. If we look at these roles encased in messages of scarcity and deprivation, we see some additional dynamics. The "hero" child will often grow up hearing messages such as work hard and save for a rainy day. They usually get their first job at a very young age. Heroes also believe that whatever they get must be shared and that they should give gifts. Certainly they don't have a choice in the matter. To choose when to gift give would be viewed by the hero as selfish. At the same time, heroes rarely receive because someone else needs or deserves it more. A hero will choose a career based on how much they can earn as opposed to whether or not its something they actually like to do. Once in a job, a hero will remain loyal and become very perfectionistic. He or she will have a difficult time understanding why after all of his hard work, someone else gets the desired pay raise or promotion. The hero readily assumes they must not have deserved it after all and will proceed to try harder while seething inwardly with growing resentments. Another powerfully ingrained message is if you have children you will have to sacrifice for them and do without. The children's needs become what is most important. Heroes also know it's not acceptable to take a vacation if you have bills to pay. For the hero, money has power. Horrible things may happen at any moment, so you had better be prepared. Work hard, struggle to get what you need, then give it to others. They deserve it more. Often these beliefs are reinforced by strong religious messages. The hero becomes altruistic in his giving and gains a great sense of pride in how little he or she can live off of and how much is so generously contributed to others. The guilt that pervades with having and being thought of as selfish forces the heroes hand in and out of his or her pocket over and over again. The guilt only subsides when there is nothing left. No consideration is ever given to spending on oneself. Others deserve it more. Operating out of all these messages, it is not surprising that the hero becomes a leader, a professional, and chooses a caretaker's occupation. Many become doctors, lawyers, or enter into other "helping" professions. Later on in recovery heroes may become self employed, happier in what they do, but constantly fighting the workaholism and old messages of "I really don't deserve."

Scapegoats take a different approach based on the messages they have received. In many ways, a scapegoat hears "we really don't expect you to ever make it." More than once a scapegoat gets told "you'll never amount to anything." As a result they become defiant, angry, and envious. While a hero child knows better than to have wants and dreams, the scapegoat not only believes he deserves good things but also believes it is owed to him. It is not uncommon for a scapegoat to be asked "who do you think you are?" The scapegoat, however, believes he is entitled. He or she learns, too, very quickly that if they have enough money, they can buy themselves out of any situation. The best money is easy money. Scapegoats also expect to be rescued and get a thrill out of living on the edge. They become under-responsible and as a result are waiting to be fired or found out. They will defiantly challenge authority and take pride anytime they feel they "got over" on someone. Scapegoats are pros at manipulating others. It's not surprising that they become compulsive spenders. Frequently, the getting and spending of money focuses around an addiction. Occupationally,when employed, scapegoats make great salespeople. They frequently do best, however, in self employed endeavors. More often than not a scapegoat is told they are "lazy and good for nothing." Professionally , though I can actually say I have never met a "lazy" person. What I have seen is that fear of failure and looking stupid can often present a so called lazy impression. Being lazy is often a perfectionist way of covering up tremendous fear and acting as if it doesn't matter.

The lost child is the quiet, invisible one in the family. The lost child hears the message there is never enough. Patiently the lost child waits for his or her turn, the time of plenty for everyone. Often though for the lost child it means "settle for whatever you can get." The lost child believes that "crumbs are better than nothing." Living in a fantasy world, the lost child relies heavily on magical thinking and is certain that someday the prince (or princess) will come. Then, everything will be better. The lost child has no sense of his or her own power and works hard at convincing themselves to just be content. Accepting broken promises becomes the norm. Self pity is part of everyday living. The lost child has no voice. It rarely occurs to them to ask for what they want. If it does cross their mind, the fear that accompanies the idea feels too overwhelming to move beyond. It is easier to be patient and just wait for someone else to be responsible in getting it for them. It is no coincidence that lost children work alone. Their careers are often isolated or quiet undertakings. Lost children professionally become great artists, academicians, research scientist, computer operators, and librarians.

The family mascot hears the message "charm will get you everything." If I am cute enough, or talented enough, I'll be taken care of and my needs will be met. The mascot hears that "it's just as easy to fall in love with a rich man/woman as a poor one." It is not uncommon for others to frequently ask a mascot "what are you going to do with your life?" Mascots never really feel grown up. As one client has described it, "I constantly feel like a kid in a grown up body." Mascots are notoriously irresponsible. Money is for play. Commitment becomes a real problem in many areas, but particularly with jobs. The mascot is a great party planner. Professionally they strive for money and recognition as athletes, entertainers, or by performing in the theater.

Inside each of these adult bodies, there is an inner child. All this child really wants is love. The hero person will do anything to get recognized. Getting approval is as close to being loved as he or she can get. All of the love becomes conditional, based on performance, which of course is never quite good enough. Phyllis had such a need for her parent's love that she agreed to work in the family business. She was there for seven years managing and being responsible for the daily operations. She never actually received a regular paycheck. Her dad would pay her bills and give her money every now and then. Never once did Phyllis see the yearly financial reports. She could only guess at how the business was actually doing. She was trapped into a financially dependent relationship and very afraid of questioning her worth. Her father's financial fears were passed onto her, driving Phyllis to work longer hours seven days a week, all along the little girl inside of her kept screaming "what about me?" Phyllis knew she had to get out yet she was so afraid of her father's anger that it took her two years to break loose from the family messages entrapping her.

Odessa, on the other hand, was determined her family would pay for the lack of attention she got. The little girl inside of her was furious, rebellious and enraged. Odessa's anger at her father's workaholism and her mother's status consciousness defied their wealth in every way she could. Odessa found a drug addicted man and over a short period of time ran away from home, had four children, never married and went on welfare. She proudly wears her welfare badge refusing any support from her family. One wonders whom she's hurting the most on getting her revenge.

Patricia is a similar scapegoat who in her addiction to alcohol and drugs, lied her way into highly technical professional positions assuring employers she had a degree without ever offering any proof. She awakens each day wondering if this is the day she will get found out. The child inside of her lives on fear, as well as shame, embarrassed at where her disease has led her.

Many become confused about the inner child and just what he or she is all about. In recovery, some have misinterpreted the child within piece as permission to justify irresponsibility and playfulness. It is true we all need to play, but only at appropriate times and in appropriate places. Our inner child is that spontaneous, emotional, self-centered part of us that needs the adult on board to guide, direct and monitor our overall well being. Without the adult part of us overseeing the inner child, our lives can become chaotic and out of control. Much of our debting and compulsive spending is the result of the inner child wanting what he\she wants when they want it. Without the part of us to set limits and plan purchases, spending sprees run rampid. For example, Sylvia is extremely angry at her workaholic husband. But she can't tell him. Childhood messages have convinced her that expressing anger directly is wrong. She has learned to repress and hold it in. The child inside, in the meantime demands to communicate. What better way than to passive aggressively take the $6,000 income tax refund check and spend it without telling him. Afterwards, it is the adult part of us that has to clean up the mess.

Robert, too, is trapped. His house is full of antique furniture inherited from his deceased mother. To Robert, the furniture is dark, dreary and depressing. Locked into each piece are painful memories of not being allowed to play or sit on what needed to be preserved for "guests". For years now Robert has been wanting to replace the antiques with something newer, brighter, and more modern but the "should's" keep that from happening. Robert has given away his power to choose what he and his inner child want and allows what others think to dictate how his living environment will feel.

What are these messages that keep us all so stuck? Many have been handed down from the depression years and generations that had no abundance. Some of these messages you may identify as your own. In reviewing the following lists you may see what helps to keep you from having most of what you desire.

A. Money messages often given in sometimes subtle ways:
More is better
There is never enough
It is not ok to talk about how much you make
Whatever you get must be shared
Money is power
Money is the root of all evil
Nobody ever gives you anything for free
Don't ask how much money someone has
Only men can have money, power, succeed, be somebody
Money is scarce and hard to get
Having money will solve all our problems
Don't let money burn a whole in your pocket - spend it quick
Having money is the most important thing in life

B. Career Messages
Men must work, women have a choice
Work hard - struggle to get what you need
Save for retirement - do without now
Settle for whatever someone offers you
Jobs are hard to come by, don't leave where you are
You are what you do
Your job is your "Higher Power"

C. Self Esteem Messages
Who do you think you are wanting more
Charm will get you anything
You take up to too much space
You don't deserve
Only foolish people pay full price
If I look too good, people won't give to me
It's bad to appear needy
If I'm pretty (cute) enough, I'll be taken care of
You'll never amount to anything
If I have money, people will like and admire me

D. Dreams and Wants Messages
Having wants and dreams is greedy
What a crazy idea
Wait until someone dies
There are others less fortunate than you
Finding the right spouse will give you what you want
That's ridiculous - what an absurd idea.
Don't even think about it. It's out of the question

Ignoring the inner child works no better than letting the child run wild. The workaholic adult often keeps their inner child tucked away in a box with the lid tightly in place. This can only go on for a limited period of time. Just as with any ingored child, the one within will find some way to get our attention. Usually self sabotage will then occur. Over time, the child within will begin to resist getting up in the morning. Or, a major illness resulting from pushing too hard, too long will get the inner child the time out they've been needing. When going to a job not in keeping with our inner child's likes and talents, restlessness will occur. This must be acknowledged and addressed or once again the child will act out in order to find a more stimulating, creative environment. To expect a former scapegoat to sit at a desk in a 9 to 5 job is absurd. A job that has positive excitement, challenge and a competitive edge is the only realistic solution towards becoming responsible. One such client, a recovering scapegoat is now a paramedic riding with an ambulance crew. The job meets both his adult's and inner child's needs. It perhaps will be helpful to look at some of the typical ways we can set ourselves up to sabotage whatever success we want to have.

Self sabotage may be obvious or subtle. My putting the wrong address on a workshop flyer potentially discouraged a lot of attendance and at the same time kept my lost child very safe. Some self sabotage occurs on a very concious level. Other instances may be old messages playing softly in the background of our minds. In reading the following list, you may be able to check off more than one or two behaviors that have helped to keep you stuck in pretty clear deprivation over time. It is a very cunning, powerful way of thinking that impacts just about every area of having abundance in our life.

Forms of Self Sabotage

* Quitting a job before you have another without contingency funds.
* Workaholism.
* Burnout-pushing the inner child beyond his or her limits.
* Repeatedly returning to the same line of work when it hasn't been right for you from the beginning because to try something els is too scary.
* Believing that if you go back to school you'll have to financially struggle, suffer and be poor.
* Throwing a roadblock in your own way - usually involves putting your wants and needs on hold while you caretake someone else.
* Self will, forcing things to happen.
* Never balancing your checkbook.
* Staying up until 2 a.m. when you know you have an early appointment the next day.
* Saying "yes" when you really need to say "no".
* Saying I know how when I don't so that I won't look stupid.
* Not asking for information.
* Procrastination.
* Compulsive spending.
* Who cares, tomorrow I may die thinking.
* Impulsive buying.

- Do it now.
- Don't think over decisions.
- Not getting input from others.
- Self dishonesty.
- Secrets from sponsor and others.
- Doing same thing over and expecting different results.
- Not maintaining what you have.
- Quitting before you reach your goal.
- Setting impossible goals.
- Making a list of too much to do.
- Minimizing difficulties, not asking for support.
- Setting up overwhelm.
- Not acting, being stuck, not getting beyond your fears.
- Surrounding yourself with stagnate people.
- Putting yourself in "slippery" places.
- Putting self around high pressure sales people without support.
- Settling for whatever someone offers you.
- Waiting for God to take care of it.
- Setting goals that are too low.
- Leaving the important things for someone else to do.
- Not billing for your services in a timely manner.
- Believing that there is a scarcity.
- Relying on luck, rather than planning.
- Trying to please everyone.
- Not allowing for possibilities. Dismissing new ideas as impossibilities.

- Becoming attached to what you have.
- Relying on memory rather than writing things down.
- Thinking "I'm too old."
- Believing I need to wait until the children are grown.
- Floating and bouncing checks.
- Hoarding.
- Relying on someone else to financially rescue you.
- Compulsive debt repayment.

The last of these, compulsive debt repayment may present some confusion. Our financial obligations (debts) are real and need to be honored. Our belief in "more is better" may lead us into thinking that the sooner we pay a bill off the better. This line of thinking presents perhaps the biggest form of self sabotage of them all. By compulsively sending amounts greater than what is asked for we give our creditors a tremendous amount of power over us and in turn end up debting to ourselves. As we send our money off to others, we have nothing left for ourselves and immediately go back to feeling deprived, an old but familiar state. Because we feel left without anything, the desire to spend or treat ourselves to something readily surfaces. The credit cards come out and the vicious cycle continues. Many a client has argued with me about paying off creditors with large sums to avoid interest charges. Yet, if nothing new is charged, and we make payments due as due, the balance will steadily come down and we have some cash in the meantime to utilize for our needs so that credit card use no longer becomes necessary. All of this does not mean that if an unexpected check or cash, or windfall comes in the mail that we should never apply some of it to our debts. The Debtors Anonymous program recommends the "Principle of Thirds" with regard to unexpected or additional income. In effect what this principle involves is dividing whatever the sum is into thirds - one third gets applied to debts, one third becomes savings and most importantly one third off the top is for you and your inner child to utilize in any way you want. This prevents any feelings of deprivation as well as any "all or nothing" thinking around money and debt repayment.

With self sabotage we need to be watchful and on alert for the cunning messages that will rob us of not only what we want but also of what we truly deserve to have. Overcoming some of it will require the adult part of us slowing down or setting limits on that child within who can act impulsively without any thought or planning. As the adult part of us remembers the inner child and allows for some wishes and wants in a planned way a new harmony can be achieved. Keeping the inner child too deprived sets up rebellion. Overindulging the inner child and letting that part of us run our decisions sets up disaster. What is needed is a loving adult in ourselves that is there to stand up for the inner child in knowing that we deserve all the good that a "Higher Power" wants to shower on us.

The old messages are going to die slowly as we work on a new way of thinking. Fear and scarcity thoughts may continue to resurface. Some specific situations seem to generate these fears all on their own. Job hunting, relationship searches, deadline and time crunches are just a few of the scenarios that have us thinking "there isn't enough." We get hooked quite often in spite of ourselves.

3

*" Many times I have been broke,
but I have never been poor."*
—Mike Todd

Deprivation Hooks

Self sabotage as explained in the previous chapter is not the
only factor keeping us from a prosperous and abundant life. There
are hooks that can trap, snare, and pull us down. The first of
these is:

Security vs. Risk

A client recently remarked in group therapy, "Everyone told
me that government employment was the best job to have." She
went on to say that after twelve years she hates it. What suppos-
edly made it a great job? As she stated, "security". Employers
across the board are notorious for enticing employees and promot-
ing loyalty through their "benefit and retirement packages."
Thinking scarcity and impending doom, twenty year olds emotionally lock themselves into careers thinking that is where they
will be for years to come. Salary increases and the fear of having
to start over at the bottom discourage a substantial number of
aspiring recovering people from getting anywhere. So what if the
child within us gets restless. We look to find some way to shut him
or her up. As a therapist, I've seen this work for awhile. But if the
job is not stimulating, challenging, creative, and fun the recovering person will need to medicate and anesthetize the inner child's

growing dissatisfaction. With some this means a return to alcohol, drugs or bingeing to numb the restlessness. What I have seen happen over and over again in working with clients is that when a job is not in line with one's heart's desires or one's Higher Power's will, it becomes impossible to permanently silence the inner child. As with any child when unhappy, resistance and rebellion begin to surface. Security means very little to a curious child with energy to spare. Our inner child will go to any lengths to get our attention. Refusing to get up in the morning on time for work is one sign of being unhappy. Calling in sick or dragging oneself to the office are also red flags along the way. At the other end of the spectrum, getting fired is the ultimate acting out of an inner child saying "I've had enough, this just isn't right for me." It is when the adult wants to stay comfortable and settled while the child inside is screaming, feeling bored and trapped that something has to change. For some this is a period of what I call divine restlessness; a nudging to move on to something else. When the prodding goes unheeded, the inner child will often throw or force us into action.

Have to vs. Want to

Another powerful hook that we can be caught up in is the belief that no matter what, "we have to". The amount of debting which transpires as a result of this kind of thinking puts us in a victim role that we may see no way out of. We become locked into what people will think of us. It never crosses our minds to ask ourselves if we are doing something because it is what we want to do. Thinking that job hopping will look bad on our employment record, we force ourselves to tolerate something that we know isn't right for us. One of the hardest things I ever did was quit a job after the first week, realizing I had made a mistake. That particular organization was not right for me. In one week I learned a lot about myself that I didn't previously know. I learned that I could not work in a room which had no windows and no people. I found myself moving the furniture every two days because something didn't seem right. The internal messages were saying that I should be grateful for this opportunity. The salary was good, so how could I walk away from that? The messages that played said my expectations were too high. All I needed to do was lower my standards. And of course "what would people think if I quit?" Quitting was something that "failures" did. According to my thoughts, I should have considered myself lucky to have been hired in the first place. What often happens in these instances is that we make our job our Higher Power. We become locked into a belief that it is our only source of income and abundance. We start to think there is a scarcity of jobs and employers. We listen for the unemployment statistics to prove and reinforce this particular line of thinking. We overlook and discount the multiple and various avenues that money and our good, can and often, is coming to us.

Another area that our "have to" thinking snarls us is in gift giving. Credit card bills are full of charges reflecting "have to" shopping for birthday, Christmas, holiday, wedding, anniversary and new baby gifts. Again, we make our decision based on what people will think if we don't agree to go along with what someone else has set as the expected office or family contribution. Without realizing it, we get caught up in gift math. Gift math occurs when we try to match dollar for dollar the cost of a present someone has given us. The question also arises over the appropriateness of giving money itself as a gift. How much is enough? Is an amount decided according to what will impress someone? Is money not given because you suspect it will make you look cheap or too lazy to shop? What has been particularly helpful to me is to give gifts to the people I care about unexpectedly throughout the year, in an attempt to completely remove the "have to" feeling and avoid the pressured times. Randomly, I send flowers once a month to someone in my life just by drawing the name of a friend, family member or business associate out of a tin can I keep on my desk. Prior to major holidays, I also create a "want to list" and a "have to list". I then look at three possible forms of giving. Some of my gifts consist of services I can offer. For example, baby-sitting, running errands for an elderly person, yard work for a neighbor, etc. Another gift I give is the gift of my time to actually be with the person. Perhaps a walk, an afternoon picnic that I provide or maybe showing up at my niece's school performance to demonstrate my pride in her accomplishments. The third form of gift giving, which I attempt to resort to less readily than before, is giving something material. When I can, I make the gift. Food, crafts, or a plant I have nurtured from a root cutting are some ideas that have worked quite well. I have found that gift giving, when using one's imagination, does not have to be the result of an obligation that causes me to debt.

Time Debting

When we are caught up in our "have to" thinking, time debting to ourselves is frequently the end product. Time debting to ourselves occurs when we have given away all of our time and received little or nothing of value in return. Quite often it involves saying "I can", when in truth we really can't. As co-dependents we continuously time debt to ourselves by putting others wants and needs first without any consideration of our own. Over scheduling and putting ourselves under excessive pressure, usually doing something we don't really want to be doing in the first place, is one of the more obvious forms of time debting. But there are many more subtle ways. We time debt to ourselves when we work overtime and don't get paid. It also occurs when we are told we can take comp time to make up for our additional hours, yet never do. Some of us even go so far that we deprive ourselves of the time it takes to meet our most basic needs, such as going to the bathroom. We hurriedly rush from one thing to the next, giving others the power of dictating where we are supposed to be and how much is supposed to be done. We lose sight of the fact that we are in charge of how we spend each 24 hours. Who among us has not stayed on the phone when someone has called dying to chat and interrupted something else we may have wanted to be giving our attention to. Another example of time debting, which includes financial debting, is signing up for a semester of school and then not showing up for class or dropping out without good reason before we are through. We may time debt by oversleeping as a way of avoiding what our fears really don't want us to pursue. Procrastination is time debting to oneself by not doing things on time and spending endless energy beating ourselves up or worrying about potential consequences. Mailing bills late, gift buying only at the last minute, postponing homework or household chores, not getting film developed promptly, all pile on the pressure.

Other very basic ways we time debt concern health and personal needs. We debt with our time when we have a personal goal, talent or interest, but can find no time to attribute to it. Not having time for relaxation and things of a spiritual nature contribute to our self debting. Not taking vacations says we don't count. Eating meals on the run, not going for routine physicals and medical check-ups, no time for a daily exercise routine, overworking and undersleeping all have the potential of being self abusive and damaging to our well being. The need for setting limits with ourselves and others is constant if we are to free ourselves from this time debting trap. A very useful question I ask myself when feeling pressured by others needs over my own is, "will anybody die if I don't...." Most of the time the answer is no and I can include taking care of myself and some of my needs along with others. In recovery, self caring is very different from being selfish. Self caring is when I take both your needs AND my own into consideration before making a decision and I am open to compromising. Selfish is when only my needs count and I not only don't want to hear your needs, but I refuse to bend in helping you meet them.

Time Debting to Others

We not only time debt to ourselves but may engage in time debting to others. This can happen when we spend too much time on the phone with friends or family when we are at work and are expected to be doing our job. It also occurs when all of our time is spent at work and not enough at home with family or friends. Not returning library books or rented video tapes on time promptly debts others who desire access of these. Any time we keep someone waiting due to inconsiderate lateness we debt another's time.

Time Wheel

For an accurate picture of any time debting you may be doing take out two sheets of paper and draw a circle on each. Use the first circle to represent your time and how it was spent over the last week. Dividing the circle into pie- shaped sections, designate how those 168 hours were used. If you slept eight hours each night, then approximately 1/4 of your circle will be designating sleep. If you worked 50 hours another fourth of the circle will be labeled work. Include pie pieces representing recreation and relaxation, time with friends and loved ones, exercise and/or any health related appointments or activities, as well as the hours spent doing chores, driving your car and necessary errands that you were engaged in over your previous week. If you need to review your calendar or appointment book to help you recall just where your time went that is fine. Once finished this circle, use the second piece of paper to designate how you would like to be dividing up your time. Create the ideal time wheel for yourself that reflects a balanced life, without overgiving time to others and undergiving your time to yourself. Then place the two circles side by side and get a picture of how far off your previous week was from your ideal. Working towards changing the picture will put you back in charge. Certainly whatever is most important to you should not reflect the smallest piece of the pie. The key to avoiding time debting to yourself is remembering that you and your needs are important, too. Every day we are given the gift of life and a new 24 hours is ours to orchestrate. Acknowledging this gift and asking for guidance and direction from a Higher Power on how best to use it will reap us many rewards. It may be that in order for us to receive those rewards, we will need to create some time gaps. Allowing for some unstructured open time is necessary. Some of us may find this extremely difficult to accomplish. If so we may want to get ourselves a time sponsor. This is a person with whom we can make contact by phone each morning and either commit that certain hours will be our open time for the day; or simply report the plans for how our day is to be spent to assure manage-ability of our schedule. Persons who are struggling with workaholism can use a time sponsor to commit a maximum number of work hours for the day or a total not to be exceeded for the week. It may be necessary to engage in a period of time recording by writing down how your time is used. This will serve to heighten awareness, particularly if there are gaps on your time wheel. We can plan better use of our time by reviewing our time recording, time wheels, and utilizing a time sponsor to reduce our time debting imposed stress. However, with all of this addressed, time debting is not the last of the deprivation hooks. Emotional debting occurs as well.

Emotional Debting

Emotional debting is very much the result of the have to thinking and behavior. Any situation that leaves you feeling obligated to someone else wherein usually a resentment grows, is considered emotional debting. Saying I am fine when I am really angry is emotional debting by not being honest. Emotional debting to oneself occurs when you don't allow yourself to have dreams or goals. It is happening at those times when your mind chatter talks you out of taking a risk and going for a vision that feels important to you. By talking ourselves out of trying, we prevent ourselves from having the increased good and abundance we deserve.

Emotional debting may also occur in our relationships with others. Parent/child relationships, spouse or date relationships and employer/employee relationships can all be loaded with emotional debting issues. As an example, in my work with others, a client shared that she felt trapped in staying at a job she hated. The reason for this is that her boss, in rescuing her, had co-signed a car loan for her. Being afraid of angering him by quitting and possibly losing her car, she felt emotionally forced to stay another three years until the loan was paid off. In the meantime her resentments grew, interfering not only with her job performance but also her emotional well being.

Lending and borrowing money from family and friends creates more than financial debt. It creates a power and control situation which easily spills into arguments and victim-like feelings. The person lending is always in control, with expectations of you accompanying this loan. You now owe them, not just financially, but emotionally. You feel less than and indebted. As the person borrowing, you get to emotionally feel inadequate and may even find yourself being reminded of your shortcomings by whomever it is that you have given your power to. It may only be a pencil you have borrowed, yet by reclaiming it as theirs, you may feel even greater deprivation and resentment than before. Often this leads to an "if you love me hook" played by the victim. A test is created, only to be passed by how much you give and how many times you become willing to be manipulated and rescue as proof that you care. The following list gives some additional clear examples of how emotional debting can deprive both ourselves and others.

Emotional Debting

Worrying.

Giving something with strings attached.

Manipulating to get what you want.

Letting yourself be drained by not setting boundaries.

Holding on to the belief that I'm too old.

Holding on to the belief that it's too late.

Making promises instead of waiting until you can do it.

Enabling and encouraging others to be dependent.

Overspending on a gift to impress or be liked more.

Bailing a child, spouse, lover out of a financial situation.

Asking or permitting an employer to advance you money.

Receiving a gift and feeling like I owe something in return.

Saying I love you just because someone has said it to you.

Not going for your vision or dreams.

Not doing something that will help you grow emotionally.

Feeling like you owe people favors.

Quitting work and expecting the person you live with to support you.

Saying I care and then not putting any time or effort into the relationship.

Ignoring an issue and hoping it will go away.

Not being honest - cheating.

Not doing what I really want to be doing.

Date debting (having sex with someone because they paid for your meal).

When emotional debting occurs there are expectations and often feelings of shame, and at some point anger, when the debtor can't meet the demands of the one in control. A true example of such a situation exists with the son of a billionaire who reports having $3.8 billion. As part of his wealth, the Dad owns 406 acres that he rents to his son. The son's rent is based on his weight which happens to be a big concern of Dad's. The son weighs about 200 lbs. Dad believes his son should weigh 182 1/2 lbs. Any month that the son is over 182 1/2 lbs he needs to pay 26% of his gross income in rent. If he is under, his rent is only 22% of his gross income. The rental agreement has become a way for dad to exert his will and judgement regarding a totally unrelated issue over his son. It is not uncommon for money to be used as a way of trying to manipulate and control what we want another person's behavior to be. People can become very focused on trying to change another person, and use money as the bribe. This kind of giving is never a gift. With emotional debting you can feel the hooks. While they are not tangible to the eye, you know they are there. They are often conveyed verbally by words such as "after all I've done for you." Sometimes these hooks are unspoken but are reflected in eyes shaded with disappointment in you. The pressure is there. You feel it. When emotionally debting, your own needs and wants are put aside and you dangle from strings that someone else is holding. Emotional debting occurs whenever the emotional development of ourselves or another become thwarted.

Cinderella Fantasy

It is not surprising, having grown up in dysfunctional families, that a number of us cling to the belief that a rescue for us is right around the corner. Soon, all will be well and we will be fine. There are one or two ways we can be hooked by this magical thinking. Some of us will identify with Prince Charming believing that if we just do more and try harder (so what if we are time and emotionally debting to ourselves) we will accomplish "happily ever after" for everyone. What we are rarely told in the storybooks is that Prince(ss) Charming suffers from stress related illness and is on the brink of physical and emotional exhaustion as a result of his search. But, he or she believes that it will be worth it in the end. Prince(ss) Charming waits patiently for his or her needs to be met and knows that someday all these efforts will truly be appreciated.

Cinderella, on the other hand, works hard at being the perfect victim. Rarely does she suffer in silence and often feels the world owes her. She waits and expects her Prince to come. It never occurs to her that she can leave her troubles and woes. She makes the anticipated Prince her Higher Power and becomes angry when things don't go her way. The idea of self responsibility and creating her own destiny through action is not something she readily embraces.

Other fantasies develop out of deprivation thinking and become the total focus of everyday living. Waiting for the check that we are sure is in the mail is a common trap. Believing that today I will buy the winning lottery ticket and it will take care of everything is another way of deluding ourselves temporarily. Waiting for rich Uncle Fred to die or Mom and Dad's inheritance, keeps us living in the future as opposed to the here and now. For some, the fantasy is that someday I'll leave my job and someone else will be there to take care of me. The reality is that there is no magic solution. The only real solution begins with a change in our thinking. As Marcia Perkins-Reed states, "maturity is reached when we realize that no one is going to come to rescue us." Wealth is not a mater of luck, chance or coincidence. Relying on luck or chance eliminates faith and removes any sense of personal responsibility. With a little planning and self discipline, we can change our luck. Waiting for Prince Charming, God or anyone else to take care of it will keep us stuck.

Giving Our Power Away

Whenever we look to someone or something else as the solution, we give our power away. Inevitably, because no one else can read our minds or really give us what our heart's desires, we end up feeling deprived. As the Big Book of AA states, "there is no easier, softer way." It is up to us to trust our intuition and make the choices that seem best for us as individuals. If we wait until we are offered a pay raise and never ask for one, we may cheat ourselves out of potentially available money. When we fail to negotiate how much time we are willing to invest in an activity with another, we give our power away. At times when we allow our children to dictate to us what their bedtime is going to be, we also let go of our power while time debting to ourselves in the process. Any time we wait for a reminder from our dentist concerning a dental checkup or a reminder regarding our car maintenance, we deprive ourselves. Waiting to be asked out by someone we are attracted to can eliminate the possibility of a date. Waiting always puts the other person in charge. Asking, negotiating and stating our preferences are active ways we can hold onto our power and decrease the lack that has appeared in our lives. It sounds easy, yet for most of us, it has been our fear that gets in the way.

We live in a world that teaches us anxiety, worry and fear. Fear is our greatest enemy. Fear in recovery is more pronounced than any other emotion. It is the root of all our addictions and at the very foundation of our anger. Ask recovering people why they settle for less than they deserve and the reasons can be summed up in fear. Fear of the unknown, fear of rejection, fear of not deserving more, fear of being greedy and selfish, fear of what others may think, fear of failure, fear of looking foolish, fear of change, fear of letting go of what we already have, fear of not knowing what we want and often the fear of getting what we want, and then not knowing how to handle it.

When we are afraid, we usually pick that time as the time to play it safe. As a result, rather than maximizing the use of our potential, we focus on how we can best get out of the situation with as little loss as possible. Cus D'Amato, a legendary boxing trainer once said, "Heroes and cowards feel exactly the same fear. Heroes just react to fear differently." None of us really know what the limits of our potential are. We cannot wait for the fear to disappear. We need to do it scared! A client once confessed he had been waiting for the fear to leave. It had not occurred to him to undertake the endeavor while in the fear. Even with heart pounding and stomach queasy, we need to just do it scared. We need to feel the fear and do it anyway.

When in our various states of fear, we may feel anything from anxious to panicked and desperate. Our fears may become so ominous that we choose to stay exactly where we are rather than approach and begin to dismantle them. We literally give them all our power. Perhaps the worse of all recovery fears that I have experienced is that which brings with it paralysis. The messages "that's impossible", "I could never", "It just won't work", seem to smack us in the face every time we clearly hear our Higher Power's will for us. I'm sure you've been there. An idea or thought comes and the very notion of it feels overwhelming. We become stopped in our tracks like an animal suddenly startled by man. Words won't come. Our minds refuse to operate. If we do speak we don't even remember what we said. Our whole body seems to stop operating, except for the sweat glands. They make up for everything else and begin to work overtime. Any self-confidence we once had is gone. We become convinced we are the most hopelessly inadequate specimen of the human race that ever existed. Breathing, which in the past we took for granted, all of a sudden becomes a highly laborious act as a result of fear. It is our fear that stops us from being happy, joyous and free. It can keep us prisoners. It can create a lethargy which we can't seem to get beyond. Fear has us rationalize our wants away. It convinces us that even our needs are really unnecessary. Our fears override any sense of reason. They are supported fully by our negative thinking and based on the principle of scarcity.

How can we get beyond our fears? When asked about his courage, the great 17th century French General Vicomte De Turenne replied, "I conduct myself like a brave man, but all the time I'm afraid. I don't give in to the fear, but say to my body, `Tremble, old carcass, but walk!' And my body walks." There may be setbacks, but don't stop. Remember a challenge that you have previously overcome and know that you will conquer again. Arthur Gordon says we can overcome fear by being bold. "Boldness is a deliberate decision to bite off more then you are sure you can chew. You know you'll have to deliver - or else. And unless you are hopelessly unqualified, you will deliver. Your pride, your competitive instinct, and your sense of obligation will see to it that you do." We need to acknowledge our fears but not coddle them. Walk with them rather than run from them. Gordon also states that "Tension (which 9 times out of 10 is based on the memory of past failures) can be reduced or even eliminated by the memory of past success." It is our fear that keeps us in a cage rather than free-falling with God. The tragedy is not what we suffer in being deprived, but what we miss in not having experienced abundance.

PART II

4

Abundance

How often do you hear about the prosperity and abundance in the world? Chances are not frequently. The only times I can recall are when the TV is announcing it's annual Publishing Clearing House winners. Do you know who the richest woman in the world is? Some of you may have suspected (and rightly so) that it is Queen Elizabeth, who reportedly has over 11.7 billion dollars. Which country has the greatest number of billionaires? According to *Forbes Magazine* (July 23,1990), it is the United States having 99 billionaires. Japan followed having 40, with West Germany having 38 billionaires. By the way, Switzerland has six and India and Venezuela each have one. It was in September, 1982 that *Forbes Four Hundred* was published for the first time. At that time, Daniel Ludwig had the richest fortune estimated at $2 billion. The poorest person on the list had a mere $91 million. In 1990, John Kluge was at the top of the list with $5.6 billion. Donald Graham, was the last on the list, with a reported $260 million. Wealth has not been declining. It is still out there. *Money magazine*, however, did a survey to find out who Americans view as rich. Ironically, the results showed that practically everyone thinks that no one in America is rich. In surveying families with an average income of $66,000, 94 percent did not consider themselves rich. Two-thirds said they want to be. But only one third actually think they ever will be. A large number, 44 percent surveyed, said that the income needed to be between $100,000 and $200,000 to be rich and 46 percent said that having over $300,000 is considered to be wealthy. So, in spite of the fact that America has over 65,000 millionaires, we believe in scarcity and that there are only a chosen few. It frequently comes as a surprise for my clients to hear that there are over 200 new millionaires every day in the U.S. If we look closer at some of these statistics, we see that Yale University has the most millionaire graduates, with Bryn Mawr University having the most female millionaire graduates. Most of the U.S. millionaires live in New York, with Washington, D.C. being second. These two locations are followed by Potomac, Maryland, Connecticut, Illinois, with Betheseda and Chevy Chasc, Maryland close behind. The place where you are least likely to find millionaires is Wyoming; a state that recently only had four. But, believe it or not, prosperity and abundance is all around us. Notice as you are reading these statistics, the messages presently running through your mind. Is there a part of you that wants to counter these numbers with poverty citations? Perhaps your thinking has you feeling just a bit cynical and argumentative at this point in time. It's OK. It is probably totally new for you to look at the reality of abundance. We have been so accustomed to thinking in terms of scarcity.

In 1991 there were 600 new porsche 911's coming in to the United States. Prior to their arrival, each one had been sold at $95,000. Perhaps one of our country's youngest millionaires is Macaulay Culkin, who at age 12 gets $5 million for his performance in the movie Home Alone Two. In spite of the abundance though, he reportedly gets a $5 a week allowance. It is rumored that his parents have him saving for a rainy day. Christina Onassis, the young daughter of Athina Onassis, gets a yearly allowance of $4.25 million. Again, it may help you to reflect on the childhood messages you got about money while you, too, were growing up.

The truth is, there is no real lack in the universe. There never has been and never can be. Edwina Gaines speaks of a woman banker who wanted to know just how much money exists in the world. After several years of study and research she found that there are enough financial resources for each and every person alive to have four billion dollars. Who has yours? You need to believe that it exists before you can imagine having it. You need to imagine having it before you can draw it to you. There is an overflowing abundance in the universe. The resources of a loving Higher Power are unlimited and every person can have access to these. Joseph Murphy in Your Infinite Power to Be Rich states "there is enough fallen fruit on the ground in the tropics to feed all of the hungry in the world." The well being of the world lies in the ingenuity of the people caring enough to distribute it.

Less than two months ago, I returned from my most recently created vision that came out of nowhere. Last April, I received a letter in the mail asking me if I would be willing to be part of a delegation that would travel to the Baltic States and assist some of the newly independent countries of the former USSR establish policy and care for the children there. Of course my first response was no way. I always said I would never go to a country where I didn't know the language. My fears jumped to the surface, at the mere thought of such an idea. Prior to the letter arriving I had been wanting to travel, and even recall asking my Higher Power to give me some ideas on where to go. This idea was absurd and out of the question. It wouldn't go away. Every time it surfaced I had a new reason for not going. Money came up as a certain reason to dismiss the idea. The trip was to be paid for by each delegate and amounted to approximately $5,000. No way could I afford that. Ultimately, having worked my third step of the AA program, I knew that I had turned my life and my will over to the care of a Higher Power. So I resigned myself to praying for guidance and help in knowing what was meant for me. The answer came as it usually does when I least expect it. I was in a movie theater watching the Babe Ruth story. When Babe went back to the orphanage to give out boys shoes, remembering the times he didn't have any, I knew that I was going to the other side of the world to visit a place I never, ever imagined visiting. I came home from the movie, filled out my paper work, and put it in the mail. Three months had passed since I received the letter. My Higher Power knows that it takes me awhile to get past the multitude of fears and trust. My real reasons for going there were really summed up the following Sunday as I attended a fourth of July service in Washington, D.C. The words that I heard were that as Americans, we are one of the youngest countries in the world and in 200 years have acquired the greatest abundance there is. I was going to the Baltic States to give back some of what I have. That Sunday, I also heard that the children are the future of the world. I knew at that point that I was truly on my Higher Power's path. By the way, the $5,000 I needed came in very surprising ways. When I thanked the minister and told her where I was going, she said that the church couldn't go with me but would love to support me financially in my endeavor. I also got a very unusual teaching offer when I bumped into my college professor whom I hadn't seen for 12 years. The money clearly was not the issue. Fear and limited thinking were the only things that temporarily got in my way. Once I was willing, I was shown the way.

Admitting that you want to be prosperous is mentally and emotionally healthy. Beauty and freedom result when we allow ourselves to be prosperous. When we are sick, we do not expect or accept that our lives should be lived that way forever. Nor should we believe that if we experience lack and deprivation that we should expect and accept that as good as it will get. There is nothing wrong with becoming a financial millionaire. There is no need to be embarrassed or ashamed of such desires. We are meant to live life abundantly. What is meant by this is quality not quantity. The real measure of our riches is in how many blessings we have that we can count. Everything that affects the quality of our lives is an element of our overall prosperity. It is a prosperity that includes loving relationships, health in mind and body, and a real joy of living. Good includes peace, order, courage, faith, joy, and well being. When we live an abundant life we have a reservoir of patience, strength, wisdom, courage, love, and happiness. Enough of a reservoir to solve any problem and heal any difficulty we may face. We are worthy of the very best. To achieve this, we need to consider our Higher Power's wishes for us. We need to incorporate what I call divine love into every decision we make and every action we take. When we do, whatever encouragement and openings we need will be there, as if by coincidence. We will be drawn to the best. In the process of becoming aware and awakening our spiritual natures, we will find that we will be led to all the answers, solutions, and information we need. Whether we recognize and know the channel or not, doors will open to help and encourage us. We are fully deserving and can move forward in assurance that further good awaits us. The only way we can fail is if we don't try. Anytime we try, whether we succeed or not, we are successful. We only need to think with our hearts and not our minds, no matter what the circumstances or situations, even those that seem negative. We must keep our thoughts in a positive vein. Each of us must come to believe in ourselves. We are each marvelously endowed. It is our Higher Power's will for each of us to have a happy, healthy, abundant life, rich with blessings. Our wealth does not depend upon customers\clients, economic conditions or outer circumstances. We can be prosperous when others are poor. Just as easily as we can be poor when others are prosperous. Look around and you will see; if it is true for others, it can also be true for you.

Fortunes are not the result of hard work. Fortunes are the result of rich ideas and an openness to receiving and operating on a creative level. We must develop an inner feeling of abundance before we can experience outer visible wealth. We don't have to search far to see goodness and abundance. We are living beyond our ancestor's wildest dreams. According to Alan Durning in his article, "How Much Is Enough?" The average person today is four and one-half times richer than his or her great grandparents were. One fifth of all American households have three or more vehicles. Sixty five percent of new homes built in America have two car garages. American children under the age of 13 have more pocket money ($230 a year) than do the 1/2 billion poorest people alive. Durning says that there are 32,563 shopping centers in this country which exceeds the number of high schools in 1987. Americans spend on an average six hours a week shopping and 93 percent of teenage girls vote shopping as their favorite past-time. As a result of being able to save on taxes, 10 million Americans now own two or more homes.

There is an overflowing abundance in the universe. The resources of God are unlimited, and every person can have access to these. Let's take a moment now to visualize ourselves as affluent. Imagine abundance in your life anywhere that you presently see lack. Imagine holding a check made out to you for $100,000,000 in your hand. Picture yourself writing a thank you to the source of this abundance. Visualize in your mind all the prosperity you want to have. Begin to formulate conscious choices about where you want that money to go. How would you feel and act right now if you had everything you wanted? Where would you live? See yourself doing those things today. Rehearse and make a mental movie of your new abundant life and play it in your mind over and over again. It is just as easy to imagine yourself prosperous as it is to think of yourself as poor. We cannot be in fit spiritual condition if we are worried about survival and paying the phone bill. Our Higher Power is willing to provide an abundance so that we can then begin to focus on more spiritual things. In recovery, being spiritually fit means that we have enough to share and spare. It is only when we have wealth that we can begin to see how unimportant material things really are. As long as we are feeling deprived, we will stay focused on that which we think is missing. It will become an obsession, blocking out any room for a Higher Power. One day I went into the supermarket and began to count how many kinds of cookies were there. I then multiplied that number by how many stores were in my area. I finally grasped that there is no scarcity of cookies in the universe. Until that point in time, I had to eat all that I could for fear that someday there might not be another cookie for me.

What would you do with your million? *Parents' Magazine* did a survey in October, 1990 and discovered:

71 percent would contribute a substantial amount to a church or charity;

56 percent, buy a new car;

51 percent, give money or expensive gifts to friends or relatives;

50 percent, buy a new house or apartment;

44 percent, buy a new wardrobe;

28 percent, take a trip around the world;

8 percent, give a substantial sum to Uncle Sam to help reduce the deficit;

7 percent, hire servants;

4 percent, buy a yacht;

2 percent, become a member of an expensive private club.

Most people also said they would continue to work. Fifty percent said they would work full-time. Thirty-five percent said they would work part-time. Only thirteen percent said they would not work at all. According to this poll, the majority decided that they would rather be happy and rich than just happy. To be really rich most agreed that they would need $5 million. This is not necessarily out of arms reach. Parents of the World War II generation will be putting a $6.8 billion inheritance into younger hands. By the way, if you are still looking for an alternative solution, *Fortune Magazine* states: "Marrying money is still the hardest way to earn it."

So how does one get happy, joyous, and free? The first step of course is to address whatever primary addictions there may be. It is not uncommon that one Twelve Step program will lead to another, similar to climbing a ladder with each rung taking us further away from our disease. Usually as a result of working a solid recovery program, things start to change. Life begins to come together again; maybe even for the very first time. By the second year we find that survival becomes a little easier. Some find employment and maybe even a new or better place to live. Some self esteem begins to build; we have friends again, and even money to put a little gas in our car if we own one. Life begins to get comfortable, not great but certainly better than it used to be. The idea of a Higher Power feels more real. We start to talk about gratitude and the promises of the program. Yet this new way of living still takes on a heaviness of its own. Acting like an adult and being responsible is hard work. The gifts of early recovery, while they are enjoyable, begin to weigh heavy on us as if we were carrying around a load of bricks. As a solution, we often look for someone to share our load. Relationships become the answer; a way to escape. Two still needy people come together offering a little, expecting a lot. Each person is looking to the other for a way to have the gifts without the responsibility. Forming codependent relationships is often a premature response to early recovery. Reflecting on the new good in our lives gives us a false sense of confidence that we have arrived at our destiny. These relationships, however, become only one of the ways we self sabotage.

Codependent relationships are not going to lead us to be happy, joyous, and free. A strong connection with a Higher Power will. It takes angels in an earthly form to lead us there. These recovery angels can be anyone who comes into our lives to guide, lead, direct, and support us. A prosperity angel can be someone at work, a sponsor in a twelve step program, or a stranger. An angel may also actually help you through a needed decision or a tough time. You may initially resist their help, distrusting someone's kindness to you. Accepting this support is often one of the first major risks in recovery. With support, love, and encouragement, we become willing to go into the unknown. Because they believe in us, we start to believe in ourselves, too. Even so, recovery starts to get scary. There are new gifts popping into our lives and we may not be sure where they will lead us or what might be expected of us next. With the help of our earthly angels, we begin to get closer to a Higher Power who has even more gifts for us. The dilemma that presents itself is how to accept new gifts that involve our wants, dreams, and visions when we already have good, and full lives. There is only one way. We must let go of some of the gifts we have already received without any guarantee that new good will come. It becomes an act of faith and trust. What if I let go of my house, job, car, friends? That is real risky. Will I survive? We have worked very hard in early recovery to get comfortable. It feels somewhat insane now that we have arrived to let it all go. Is there something else out there for us? Recovery from deprivation is all about letting go of what you have and opening your heart and hands for something unknown. Each accomplished vision brings with it new good. Good is never static. It is progressive. It changes and evolves. To make room for new good, we will need to release some of what we have. Over time we may outgrow some of what was once new. We can not go through two doors at the same time. We must let go of the knob of one to get to the other. In DA this concept is described as the vacuum principle. The vacuum principle states that in order for something new to come in, we often need to let go of the old. Catherine Ponder suggests making an elimination list of all the things that really need to go. She insists that spring and fall house cleanings are still a good idea. We need to let go of worn out or unused things. We need to learn to let go, give up, and release what we have to make room for what we want and desire. If we cling to what we have we will slow down or even stop all of our progress. Just like we often outgrow our clothes; we outgrow jobs, relationships, and old ways of thinking. It does not work to hang on out of fear. It is frequently healthy to move on. In doing so, we often create an opportunity for new good to enter. I'm sure there is someone who would love to have your job as you progress to a more exciting and challenging endeavor. Create a vacuum and you can be sure something new and good will come in to fill it. Should you not be convinced, clean out your closet or basement and just watch how quickly something new gravitates to the vacant space. It never fails. It is letting go of good which is a lot harder than letting go of bad. Trusting that as we let go, new good will come, requires a giant leap of faith. There is no guarantee. We know that deprivation evolves out of fear. We can only trust that abundance evolves out of faith. Our loving Higher Power has been waiting for any opportunity to shower greater and greater prosperity upon us. So often our response has been "no thanks, God. I'm really okay with what I have." Clients repeatedly hear me ask " how good can you stand it?" The only thing blocking the good is us. With every good thing that we are willing to let go of something AS GOOD OR BETTER is on its' way. Paradoxically by letting go, we get to have more and better. A very good exercise that I often recommend is for each of us to begin by taking an inventory of everything that we have. Write each item down and put an estimated dollar value beside it. Include everything! Don't forget your dog, computer, your spa or health club membership, the value of any trees you have in your yard, your talents, your children, and your education. Remember too, to include your eyes, arms, legs, and hearing. Use the insurance companies dollar value if you have trouble tabulating these on your own. As you make this list begin to become aware of all the abundance you already have. Include any sentimental items, valuing them accordingly. Once this feels somewhat complete go back over the list and put an X beside everything that you would be willing to let go of trusting that if you did something as good or better would indeed take its' place. As you probably are beginning to realize, we often become extremely attached.

We can break down any walls keeping us from our abundance, though, through the persistent use of thoughts, words and pictures of prosperity. Wealth will not come until we are mentally and emotionally ready for it.

When we are mentally in a true millionaire consciousness, we will not need to fight for our good or compete for it. It will unfold. A positive state of mind has an attracting power for prosperity and success. Money is a medium of exchange. It is nothing more than a symbol. Imagine yourself having a supply that never runs dry and see yourself using it to serve others in grand and wonderful ways. Use what you receive freely. Use it for good only. Money is good. But remember prosperity does not simply refer to the size of one's bank account. A prosperous person is a happy, well adjusted individual. When we speak of prosperity, we are referring to *all* good. Prosperity is a richness that includes wholeness of health and physical well being, an abundance of love and money, and a wealth of friends, ideas, and material goods. Anything that you can perceive, you can achieve and receive. To have, we must expand our consciousness and not only look for, but expect good. We must learn to follow our inner guidance, especially when what is before us looks impossible. Answers come by keeping a receptive attitude. What seems impossible gradually falls into place. Our good expands even beyond our imagination. We experience joy, but only as a result of having waited in faith.

5

"If one advances confidently in the direction of his dreams, and endeavors to live the life which he has imagined, he will meet with a success unexpected in common hours..."
—Henry David Thoreau

Visions

Our visions come from within. They are not goals. They are not something we have to do. A vision does not come from expectations of society or others. A vision is a dream that we dare to have. So many of us have only wanted what we have needed. In doing so we have eliminated the possibility of having so much more. We need to be told it is OK to want, to dream. The "Promises" of the AA and other twelve step programs become demonstrated when we allow ourselves to have a vision. With our visions, we are on our way to being "happy, joyous, and free." Yet, certain myths exist that often stand in the way of us holding onto our visions.

Myth #1 - The belief that visions are dreams which stand very little or no chance of ever coming true.

Myth #2 - That people with visions are dreamers, idealists who walk around with their head in the clouds.

Myth #3 - That people who have visions are the rare exceptions like Ghandi, Einstein and Henry Ford. We could never measure up to them.

Myth #4 - That we will need to sacrifice all that we have in order for a vision to come true.

Myth #5 - That we can have them become real only later on

in life after all the important things such as career success and raising a family have been taken care of.

Myth #6 - That visions must be held onto in our heads or they will fade. The truth is that visions always lie within our hearts and no one can ever take them away.

By expanding our mind beyond these myths, we discover that we can achieve any idea that we conceive. To be whatever we want to be, we simply need to go and do whatever we want to do. With a vision, we need to state it and claim it:

I want to be...

I want to do...

I want to have...

Tracey, the nursing school student mentioned earlier, created a vision of someday being able to afford a place of her very own. Both Jim and Ann wanted safe new homes where an atmosphere of shame did not prevail. Fran hoped to someday have her very own miniature golf course where people of all ages could come and play.

When any of us give ourselves permission to dream we become a living magnet drawing us to the people, circumstances, and situations that we need to accomplish our desires. We know if we are on the right path with our vision by putting it out to the universe. The universe will absolutely support us if our vision is meant to be. I knew within three months of beginning private practice that my vision was one that would meet with success. Everything I needed to do fell into place seemingly effortlessly. Office space became magically available. Clients heard about me from unknown sources. The answers to questions about running a business just came from supportive professionals. It has been very similar in writing this book. There were so many things I didn't know. Every time I thought about stopping, the universe nudged me along with unexpected offers of support, help, information, and ideas. Every trouble spot appeared to have an automatic solution totally outside of me and anything I was doing.

The best and most suited visions are the ones that pop into our minds seemingly out of nowhere. At first a vision may appear and be judged by oneself (and others, if shared) as an absurd and impossible idea. A vision may come as a sudden inspiration, a passion, or as part of an enthusiastic activity that excites you. A vision carries with it a certain amount of temptation, a personal challenge. It will enliven your mind, arouse your curiosity and creativeness, and enrich how you spend your day. It demands that we trust our heart. However, our mind may create uncertainty, indecision and hesitancy. This is where we often get deterred. As discussed earlier, we must stop such thinking. In looking at nature and non-thinking creatures, we can see that no one convinces beavers to make dams. No one shows bees how to make honey. Seagulls on the beach don't question or anxiously worry about what might be next. They instinctively know and do what they were created to do. There are no complaints from seagulls. No lamenting over how hard and difficult life is for them. They have no mind to complicate doing what they know. Whether to be on this section of the beach or further down is unimportant to a gull. What matters is that they are drawn to water and are meant to be on the beach. Where they do this is insignificant. On the other hand, we can spend days agonizing over whether a vision is right for us and never get to a point of beginning to ever find out. Perhaps if we were more like seagulls and other creatures of nature and just accepted where we are at the moment, we would then find ourselves moving forward with the assuredness of the birds. They just know. If we allow our minds to be quiet, trust our own instincts, so will we. Our actions will occur in easily, orderly ways. We will find that we act and ultimately thrive in abundance without any laborious effort.

We do not need to sacrifice to achieve a vision. Accomplishing a vision is a matter of following your bliss; allowing yourself to experience good fortune. Yet, it is not about your Higher Power giving you more. What we get from God is ideas, not things. It is true that when we take risks and follow up on our ideas, they often lead us to an abundance of good things. These often come as a result of trust and faith that no matter what, we will be all right. More then the material rewards though, fulfilling a vision is really about uncovering and releasing your own "imprisoned splendor" as Eric Butterworth so nicely puts it. Visions and dreams become real for us when we surrender and become still. They come from practicing listening to our still inner voice. We give up self will. We open our minds and listen with our heart. A vision can be anything. It may be buying a house and relocating; it may be your dream job; achieving a degree or pursuing additional education; learning how to start and manage a business or creating and developing a happy and loving relationship. It is our intuition that becomes the vehicle for communicating the path we are to take. Our divine purpose lies solely in our realization of what it is within us that we have always wanted to do, or perhaps at the present moment feel guided and led to do. Believing in our decisions, we simply need to consult with our Higher Power first and then proceed from there. So how do we go about developing a vision? In Baltimore as part of the DA program, there is a once a week Vision Twelve Step Meeting which focuses totally on having dreams come true. Fulfilling a dream of getting a pilot's license, attending art school, becoming a dolphin trainer, going to Italy, becoming a film maker, writing a first book, and getting out of debt are only a few of the talked about visions there. Some tools to be used early on, which I have found helpful, are creating wish lists, treasure maps, and prosperity affirmations.

Wish Lists

Creating a wish list may be incredibly difficult for some. The greater our deprivation thinking, the more likely we may draw a blank. It helps to sit down with paper and pencil and just allow yourself to dream. You may have material wishes, relationship wishes, travel desires, career dreams, wants regarding your health and so on. There is no limit to wishing. There is nothing selfish about having dreams and wishes. Unless we can think it, there is very little likelihood that we will create it. So just begin anywhere. If you are stuck, bring up the question among friends, "If you could have anything you ever wanted what would it be?", and brainstorm wishes. Use brainstorming to your own advantage. Not only will it give you the permission you may need to dream, but it also may give you some ideas you didn't have. Keep your wish list going. Add to it anytime a new desire comes to surface. You may also want to state your wishes out loud, not for the purpose of having the wishes granted (although that may start to happen) but, just for the practice of having them. At the same time, watch for and guard against the messages that come from within that tell you your wishes are silly or really not worth having. My mind can do a wonderful job of talking me out of all my wishes even when all I'm doing is putting them down on paper. Before I realize it, I have fallen back into being satisfied with having what I need as opposed to what I want.

After you have decided what some of our wishes are, it helps to write to your Higher Power. In your letter tell your Higher Power what you want, what you will do with it and how you will use whatever it is as a way of doing service and contributing to others. There is nothing selfish about wanting something that will materially and spiritually benefit others.

Treasure Maps

Continuing on with this process of having our visions become real, creating a treasure map can be a way of picturing the desired outcome. Once we state our wishes and verbally give them some energy, we then need to visually make them real. A clear way of doing this is with a prosperity vision book made out of a photo album or with a treasure map. Other writers, such as Catherine Ponder refer to these as Prosperity Maps or wheels of fortune. The idea of a treasure map is very similar to a road map in that it serves as a way to a destination. Treasure maps, like road maps, help us to get to what we desire. By making a map, we bring into focus our thoughts and feelings surrounding our vision. We manifest our vision visually in all of its ecstasy. A treasure map is very similar to a collage. It can be made on anything. Mary Katherine MacDougall in her book suggests even the inside of a box lid can be used to assure privacy if your vision is one you prefer to keep to yourself. Most treasure maps are done on paper, colored poster board or lightweight cardboard. What you create is what you get so be sure to use big paper if you want big results. Be careful not to overcrowd your map, or your results too, may be crowded into your life with little or no room for enjoyment. Catherine Ponder states that "according to the ancient science of color, you should carefully select what colors you use." Green or gold poster board is best for money and wealth, as well as for job and career success. Orange or bright yellow should be used for health, energy and a more vital life. Pink, rose or warm red are best representing love, marriage, happiness in human relationships and things of the heart. Blue is for intellectual pursuits and education. While white and yellow are colors best used to express spiritual desires.

Making several maps can clarify several visions you may have. You may create a map pertaining to your ideal job or business, one regarding an educational dream, health, financial prosperity, or love and friendships. One treasure map that I designed several years ago had to do with travel. As a result of achieving this vision I have thus far been to Switzerland, Ireland, Bermuda (twice on cruises), sailing, and to the beach several times. Prior to my map making I had not been anywhere other than to visit relatives in nearby states. A client recently shared with me her treasure map showing the kind of house she hopes to buy including the furnishings, landscaping and interior design.

With making the map, we express an inner faith. By visualizing our good, we can then attract it. It is important to include words and affirmations on the map to give it strength. Also, adding play money or checks assures us of the financial means to carry out the vision. Placing a spiritual symbol will give the map protection and divine direction, opening the way for abundance and good to come to you. There is no limit to the number and kinds of maps that can be made. On occasion, we may even decide to make a map for another. For example, an expected unborn child's health and happiness, world peace or a drug free community can be added to your visually displayed dreams.

After your map has been designed, it is very important to look at it at least once a day affirming that it's good is on the way. Expect the good you have captured in pictures to be yours. Thank your Higher Power for creating the good you have, and hope to have, in your life. Your treasure map is a reflection of your faith. You only need to proclaim it daily to have it be yours.

Removing Limiting Thoughts

Charles Fillmore in his writings on prosperity states "There is no lack of anything anywhere in reality. The only lack is the fear of lack in our minds. We do not need to overcome any lack, but we must overcome the fear of lack." There is abundance. What we must constantly deal with are our own thoughts that get in the way. We can change these one by one if we are persistent. In doing this, it is important to notice what we say to ourselves and others. Attaching the word "my" or "only" can hinder our progress. Many times we state "my problem is..." indicating an attachment or ownership that might suggest an unwillingness to let go of something we say we don't really want. Using "I only have" to describe our money or time reminds us and others of our scarcity, holding onto the idea of limited good. We need never postpone our good. Instead we need to express the good we want to have. If we want prosperity, think only prosperity thoughts and speak only prosperity words. Emmet Fox states "It's amazing to think how many interesting and worthwhile things most of us could do, if we had not put mental handcuffs on ourselves." As we become aware of our negative thoughts, there are things we can do to turn our thinking around. We can:

- Surround ourselves with prosperous people. Gather around energetic, enthusiastic individuals who are risk takers. Be with gentle, encouraging, warm people who support us in our dreams. Positive people who seem to have a knack for making things happen in their own lives can be a strong influence. Children and people who know how to have fun will help us reach that inner part of ourselves. As Joel Goodman states, "Hang out only with people who treat you like gold."

- Avoid angry, hostile, needy, draining, and depressed people. We have no need for abusive relationships. Supporting someone in being a victim will only deprive us of our own needed energy. Without limits on other's demands of us, there is no time to work on a vision. With some people we can easily become over-whelmed by their needs and find ourselves participating in a giving marathon exhausting our resources and receiving nothing in return.

- Listen to what others are saying. If all they talk about is the pain and tragedy that exists in the world, get away. Shut out others' reports of impending doom. Avoid news broadcasts, especially right before going to bed. Read only comics section of the paper unless checking for coupons and recipes which can add to your abundance.

- Be selective and let go of the limiting thought that we must have everyone like us or we are not good persons. All we really need are five or six people who accept us and all our shortcomings. Stop trying to be loved by all. It's impossible and far too exhausting.

- Put ourselves in positive places. Go to concerts, the park, the beach, and church if it feels right for you. Attend twelve step meetings where you hear people sharing the solution as opposed to being stuck in the problem. Step meetings are a perfect place to hear how others are using the twelve step programs to make changes in their lives. Some places have "Promises" meetings which focus on pages 83-84 of the Alcoholics Anonymous Big Book where we are told of the good that will happen as a result of our hard work. It is here that we are promised we will "lose our fear of people and economic insecurity."
(for complete list see appendix)

- Take vacations. We all need time for renewal
   and rejuvenation.

- Work on forgiveness and letting go of resentments. Forgiving is a choice. It takes courage, yet the real reason for forgiving is for ourselves. It removes a block that separates us from others and the good we wish to receive. Forgiveness frees the forgiver, and anyone who accepts forgiveness, to love and grow. Forgiveness is not easy, sentimental, condescending, righteous, or conditional. Forgiveness is purely a decision we make to move forward.

- Yell "Stop." Censor your mind, take charge of what you think. Just as we can change the TV channel, change the station in your mind. Switch from a negative or a worrisome thought to something positive and filled with aliveness. Substitute a new thought. We get to decide what we are going to allow our minds to dwell upon.

- Create positive excitement. We are excitement junkies. We have become addicted to crisis and chaos. Anything else seems boring. In recovery, we need to substitute positive excitement. If we do not go for our visions and dreams we will go back to some sort of crisis just to feel alive. It is time for us to get our adrenaline rushes from our accomplishments, not our failures. Going for a vision is all about trying something new. Go for it!

What can we substitute for our old negative thinking? What follows is a list of some prosperity affirmations I have gathered and shared with others. My favorite affirmation is "I don't have to struggle to get what I need." Hopefully, you will select one or two that may help develop your vision, say it on a daily basis and have all that you dream become a joyous reality. Tape some of them to your bathroom mirror and recite them while you brush your teeth or shave. I have some over my kitchen sink for when I am standing still and washing dishes. Another good place is on the dashboard of your car or on your desk, framed and in a noticeable place. It is especially helpful to pick one and use it as a thought to go to sleep by. Repeating a positive statement over and over as you drift off in slumber makes going to sleep easier and worry free. It also ensures all your dreams will come true. Just like learning our A,B,C's affirmations need to be repeated over and over and over again. Affirmations can be said, sung, and even turned into games. They can be traded with friends and used as the thought for the week. As easily as the A,B,C's have become a part of our lives, so can learning the words of positive thinking.

Prosperity Affirmations

I am now attracting all of my good to me.

All that I give circulates back to me with great speed.

As I allow myself to feel grateful, I have more to feel grateful for.

I am filled with prospering ideas that are manifesting good in my life today.

I give thanks in advance that all my needs are being met.

My life is becoming more enriched everyday.

Right decisions come easily today. I release all concern and fear that keeps me from my good.

I joyfully share all of my good news with others.

It is safe for me to turn away from the familiar to attain all of my visions.

I now move forward in a spirit of excitement, enthusiasm and expectancy.

As a child of God, I deserve all of the best.

A time for rest enriches me.

I am renewed and inspired as I go forth.

I release all negativity and sense of lack.

I am filled with joy as I count my blessings and make way for more.

I live in a prosperous place.

The world is my playground and I frequently travel to new and fun places.

Some additional affirmations include:

There is an abundant supply of courage and strength for any undertaking that faces me.

I believe today that the answers will come.

I am open to guidance and direction from my Higher Power.

I am accepting of any and all good that comes my way.

I am free of all doubt and fear.

Freely I give, freely I receive.

I have the strength to go forward even when filled with doubt and fear.

I choose to be happy and have fun in all I do.

Not my will, but thy will be done today.

I am filled with prospering ideas that enrich my life.

I am instilled with confidence and am being guided on my way.

I am a messenger exemplifying the good available to all.

It is OK for me to exceed my parent's limitations.

I am open to expected and unexpected sources of income.

I attract and radiate good in all I do.

I am not my debts; I am a person of wealth.

Who I am is not a reflection of what I have.

If anybody can do it, anybody can do it.

I was not created to be a failure.

All that limits me is now being removed.

Miracles happen when I act on my dreams.

All things are possible.

I think calmly and act wisely.

I am a person of worth.

My job is not my Higher Power.

I am open to receiving.

I can have unlimited money at any time.

I am receiving love in all forms.

I am physically, emotionally, and spiritually abundant.

My Higher Power is the source of all good.

I prosper more each day.

Nothing is too much to ask of God.

No one has to have less for me to have more.

Divine love blesses and multiplies all that I am, all that I give and all that I receive.

Having a clear picture of our vision, we can now begin the process of making our dreams a reality. We begin by having trust and moving forward into whatever fears may lie ahead. By now, having worked hard at changing our fear based thinking, what I usually hear from others is "I can't afford it." Whatever the vision entails, inevitably lack of money becomes an issue. There are tools to help us get beyond this limitation. It is true that if money is the only problem, then there really is no problem. "Seeding" money may be part of our answer.

6

*"Sow a thought; reap an action.
Sow an action; create a destiny."*

Seeding Money

The concept of seeding money in order to generate more may sound strange at first. However, the seed money principle is both scientifically and spiritually based. In effect what this principle means is that money seeded multiplies. Scientifically, money has energy. Spiritually, it can be viewed as God in action. It has the potential of doing good. Yet when hoarded, money serves no purpose. If treated as a buried treasure it becomes dead and does no one any good. Paradoxically, by using and spending money non-impulsively, we open ourselves up to even greater abundance of spiritual and material things.

How does seeding money work? First, we decide upon an amount that we would like to have multiplied by ten times for any reason whatever. We then give our seed money to a person, church, hospital, school, service agency, or charity that relies on donations. This may be done anonymously as a way of insuring some degree of humility and keeping our ego out of the way. Giving to some place or someone who serves as a source of inspiration to us will benefit us the most. I am often inspired by people who fight to overcome some hardship on a daily basis. It is to them that I seed. It also works to give it to a friend or even a stranger. Once "planted" our seed money will return ten times. We simply must have faith and maintain an air of expectancy, noting for ourselves any expected or unexpected money that comes to us. As stated by Dr. Jon Speller, " 'The Law of Tenfold Return' always works." Remember the source of all good is your Higher Power. There is no scarcity in the universe. If you doubt and don't believe you will get your return, you won't. Doubt interferes in creating results. Taking chances and hoping it will happen won't work either. The only thing that can limit what you receive is your beliefs. Your thinking alone affects what you get. "There is no Divine limitation, only our human one," states Jon Speller. Remember, too, that money is only a medium of exchange. What you acquire or do with it is what's important, not the money itself.

There are many forms and expressions of wealth in addition to cash. Manifesting cars, trips, jobs, airline tickets, clothes, and unexpected opportunities can all be demonstrations of planted seed money. The underlying working of seed money principles relies on trust. This is brought to our attention as we notice that printed on the U.S. dollar bills is "In God We Trust". When we allow for the possibility that anything can happen, we will be open to our good coming from many avenues. As Robert Russell states, "instead of thinking, I can't afford it...let us think, in God We Trust." If we fear we will lose what we have, whether it be money, job, or material things, we will. What we think is what we get. There is no lack of supply, only a lack of asking. We need to claim what we want and not stay focused on what we don't want. If we believe in our own success, we will create it. So often we look around us for evidence of others who have achieved or enhanced their richness. We want to know the odds. This is all right. Yet, we need to remember we can go beyond what already seems possible. That which comes to us will be exactly what we are mentally and emotionally prepared to handle. We need to put ourselves in prosperous places so that we can begin to feel comfortable and thereby draw greater abundance to ourselves.

We can only become truly rich by circulating our money. Giving and receiving freely, not through hoarding. Giving with compassion and in a selfless way returns the good to us. We must give in order to receive but remember, we must also receive in order to give. In the same way that a car can take you over miles of roads when the gas tank is full, if we fail to refill we become stuck as others pass us by. Interestingly enough, clients will endlessly try to argue with me about the need to receive. Clients have shared with me in numerous instances that expecting to get something is wrong or will lead to disappointment. For many of us this is where we run into problems, not with the giving but even more so with receiving. We have become a generation of caretakers and victims at our own expense. In our distorted thinking, our low self esteem dictates that others are far more deserving than we. Without realizing it, we jump on the speeding train of self debting. We give our time, our health, our money, our talents and our very own spirit away, refusing any well intended and often Higher Power sent good in return. In our striving for independence, we have become overly self reliant as opposed to reliant on a Power outside and greater than ourselves that wants us to have good.

I need to state over and over that it is not only OK to expect to receive, it is necessary. We have the right to be given to. We are persons of worth. Our talents, our services, our ideas, our giving deserves to be acknowledged, validated, and supported in very real and tangible ways. It is OK for all of us to get our share. There is enough. Seeding money gives to others. It is only natural that others shall give back to us. Money that we seed is a way of saying thanks in advance to a Higher Power for that which we shall receive. Seeding differs from the idea or concept of tithing. When we seed we take a bigger risk. We are anticipating something will come as a result of our faith and action. With tithing, we are saying thanks after the fact by giving back a portion of what we have already received.

After doing a workshop where I introduced the seeding idea, my words were met with great skepticism. Personally knowing that seeding works, I did not feel offended. The suggestion was made to the audience that if they were willing to, give seeding a try. Any amount given to any source of spiritual inspiration would be fine. I asked if anyone did seed to keep in touch and let me know of any results. The workshop was on a Saturday. By Tuesday messages started pouring in. One woman seeded $1.50 to a home for battered women and the next day received a $4.50 check from a secondhand shop for clothes she had given them to sell on consignment over two years ago. She was continuing to expect the $10.50 balance from other sources at the time of her call but couldn't wait to share the surprised good that had already come. Jim seeded $5 to AA (Alcoholics Anonymous) and received a call asking him to fill in and teach a class for a $50 fee. Since he hasn't taught in over 15 years, he was quite surprised by this unexpected offer. Susan seeded $10 and received a $100 refund from the phone company, not knowing that she was due this. Andrea seeded $10 and three days later was offered an art school scholarship of $1,000.00. Prior to coming to the workshop, Ann was given a cost of $800 for car repairs she needed. She decided to seed $80 as she left. Upon picking up her car, she was given an adjusted bill of just $32. No other money was needed. My own experience that day involved seeding more than what actually felt comfortable. The bigger the risk, the bigger the gain. Being inspired by my audience, I seeded anonymously back to them $100. Due to my own scarcity thinking I have always had a hard time letting go of money, particularly what I view as a large sum. However, I knew the risk would be good for me. On Wednesday following the workshop, I received a phone call offering me a consulting job that would pay me $1,000. Sometimes there are things in recovery that when I take action just happen and there is no real way for me to explain them. This was just one of those times. Having seeded, we only need to look for our good to manifest itself. Accomplishing our visions can now be under way.

Farming

As a child, I spent many hours at my grandparent's farm. My family also lived in a rural area where chickens, cows, rabbits, pigs and calves were a common sight. It was a necessity as well as an accepted part of life to supplement the family income with home grown products. Fruits, vegetables, eggs, milk and dairy products were provided by nature as opposed to today's modern supermarkets. During those years, what I learned about farming laid valuable foundation for a path out of deprivation.

Farming as I know it today is a simple matter of taking a very tender, delicate seed and bringing it to fruition. This requires care, commitment and of course hard work. In order to obtain a seed, we must be still and open our mind in the same way we would open an outstretched hand. It is not up to us to question why one particular seed has been given to us and not someone else. We don't even really need to know what the seed will look like once it blooms. We simply must be open to whatever shape or form the seed takes, trusting that it is meant to be placed in our care. We need to be very careful we do not discard our seed. In our everyday busied lives we toss away countless ideas that if planted would gladly take root in spite of our thinking of them as impossibilities.

Sowing

Once we have acknowledged and accepted the seed given to us, we then must prepare for planting. It is now that time and place are of utmost importance. Trying to plant during a snowstorm or blizzard will only be a waste of time. Trying to do too many things at once will shortfall our seeds and they may become abandoned in the cracks of life. Some visions go no further than this. Planting requires thinking ahead, gathering information on what it will take to have our seed idea flourish. The soil into which the seed will be placed must be toiled and very fertile. All of us know too well that seeds planted on concrete do not grow. Yet, we frequently will continue to try and force something to happen. The place where we are may not be suited for what we hope to grow. Lilies will not grow in the desert. When on the path of prosperity, nothing ever needs to be forced. If in our efforts we feel a resistance, it usually means we are headed in the wrong direction. It is best to stop and turn inward for clearer direction. Pushing will only take us further down an unfruitful path. Praying for guidance and affirming that we are inspired by divine wisdom will help get us back on the right track.

As part of accepting the seed we may need to go away, perhaps for training. Or we may need to move to a location where our talent can be watered and grow. A commitment made when accepting the seed, frequently calls for surrender of those things outside the seed. The distractions or diversions attempting to lead us away from where we need to be may feel like strong winds blowing us in far away directions. Having accepted the responsibility of the seed placed in our care and having done the ground work, we trustingly bury our seed in the appropriate place at the appropriate time.

Tending

What often follows then is a time of darkness and fighting the weeds that attempt to strangle and hold back the frail idea that wants to come forth. This is a period of time which calls for patient faith and a trusting knowingness that once having done all the necessary footwork, we will be rewarded. A child planting a seed does so with great expectancy, watching over the soil for the first sign of growth. However, this first sign does not mean total victory. The seedling requires more support and attention than before, just as does our vision. During this time there may be numerous weeds trying to suffocate and crowd it out. For us the weeds become our own negative thoughts. Thoughts such as "this is too hard; I'll never make it; what's the use" will lead us to give up on nurturing the seed. These are the weeds we must pull out and rid our seeds of before they can do any major harm. If we view what we want to reap as impossible, then our own negativity will automatically repel it from us. A client who worked as a real estate agent was experiencing great difficulty at a time when the market was reported to be down. By suggesting that she had nothing to lose by getting rid of the negative thoughts she made room for a rather substantial sale to show up in her life. Tending is a time of patient waiting, expecting, trusting that our good will come. The client had worked hard, taken action and only needed to have faith that her dreams would be fulfilled. We need to remember a gardener does not give up and fail if his flowers don't bloom the week after seeds have been planted. However, without certain tools we may feel frustrated because little gets accomplished.

Action Plans

As a tool an action plan is the primary ingredient in creating abundance. What we harvest will be a result of the effort we put into it and the support of a Higher Power. As stated in the booklet "Partnership" by Vincent P. Collins we are responsible for doing our one percent. Formulating an action plan helps us to clarify what this one percent is. Basically, by sitting down and listing what needs to be done we give ourselves a sense of direction. It also helps to keep us focused. Planning allows us to be in charge and hold onto our power. We can feel a greater sense of accomplishment as we go back to our list checking off the tasks as they are completed. Listing even the most minute details, steps that need to be taken, paves our way. It is important to break these steps down so that we do not feel overwhelmed. Adding a time line to the action plan further guides us in accomplishing our vision. As an example, let's say you want to change jobs.

An action list may look something like this:

Job Change
Read the classified ads

Write a resume

Get resume typed

Mail resumes out

Set up an informational interview with others who already have a job you think you might like

Buy an outfit to wear on interviews

The action plan could go on and it could be modified at any time. If we were to go back and add a time line to it, it may look like the following:

- read the classified ads - every Sunday
- write a resume - by March 14th this year
- get resume typed - within 10 days of it being written
- mail resumes out - at least 5 weekly beginning no later than April 1
- set up informational interview - prior to sending out resumes
- buy an outfit to wear on interviews - within next 3 weeks

Remember that it's perfectly all right if you do not meet the time line for one or more of your actions. The action plan is not designed to be a weapon that you use to beat yourself up with. Just the exercise of writing an action plan itself serves a major purpose in owning and becoming aware of our part in achieving the desired results. If a particular action is repeatedly postponed or meets with locked in resistance, then we need to step back and look at why that specific step appears to be too difficult for us to overcome. More than likely we have become locked into an old belief that has set us up for self sabotage. In almost every instance the resistance represents an unresolved fear.

On occasion our Higher Power's will for us and the action steps we need to take can be accompanied by intense fear. It may be gut wrenching, heart throbbing, and can include all the terror of a living nightmare. Finding the courage to confront, or ask for what we may want or need, can leave our voice cracking and our bodies immobilized. In recovery, we may experience a degree of fear that we have never even known to exist before. How do we get past it? What can we do?

Bookending

Perhaps the most valuable tool I've come across to help me achieve my vision is bookending. This tool is used a lot in the DA Program when one needs to call a creditor to negotiate an overdue payment. Or when someone needs to risk communicating their needs in a relationship yet is finding they are lacking in perhaps skill and courage. To bookend oneself, we call a safe person right before taking a fearful step and rehearse what we want to say or do. We then ask this person to be available for a return call at the end of our endeavor. We call back after completing our action, even if there was no response. Making the commitment to another person, and having their support and encouragement add to our needed supply of courage. The follow-up contact gives us someone supportive with whom to share the outcome. One particular client used this technique to help herself through a portfolio review. Others have bookended themselves with going on job interviews. Added to this technique, we may want to call on an invisible army made up of friends, sponsor, our group therapy partners, mentors, and recovering persons to mentally go with us into our fear filled situations. Closing our eyes we can visually picture the support of these loving allies standing right behind us as we face head on the roadblocks in our way.

Whether or not to take a risk or action often requires use of another tool - prayer, or as I sometimes like to think of it; positive thought. Over and over again, I use a shortened version of the serenity prayer and ask my Higher Power for courage and wisdom. I pray for guidance and direction in all my affairs. My most answered prayers are those that are short. While my life often seems complicated and involved, my requests to a Higher Power are best when clear and simple. I have found that when we can keep our minds occupied with positive and constructive thoughts, we cannot be afraid. There are two additional very simple tools to use in your farming of a vision. One involves committing on a weekly basis, aloud to others, two to three actions (big or small) that you plan to take during the course of that week to help you achieve your vision. The second is to report back the following week how you have done. This really helps to keep us focused and working on accomplishing our dream without too much time sliding by. From time to time, we do become stuck, not knowing what to do next. We can then go into our tool shed and use brainstorming with others to get us through. A very valuable lesson to learn regarding visions is that they can never be accomplished alone. Having safe, supportive people and a faith in a Higher Power make it all possible.

Reaping

It is unlikely we will make it to this point without persistence and huge amounts of support to carry us through the discouraging times. Every vision I have ever accomplished in my life has had its moments of hopelessness and total despair. Sometimes almost in spite of ourselves, we do succeed. Reaping is the end result when all that is needed has been done and we haven't given up. We can then revel in the beauty and wonder of what has come forth. This is a time of giving thanks that our efforts have not been in vain. We have permission to celebrate the growth and share in it with others. In doing this we may in turn serve as an inspiration to someone else's dream coming true. We find that we are rewarded for our action and all the labor invested. The process itself has carried rewards totally unexpected. New information, new people, new self esteem come to us regardless of any other tangible results. Not all visions turn out how we planned them. There may be and usually are surprises. It is not rare or strange that the accomplishment of one vision leads us to another.

Since the time of beginning this book, much has been accomplished by our friends in the first chapter. Tracey did in fact get past her negative beliefs and began to believe in the possibility of somehow having her own place. After creating her treasure map, Tracey began letting people know that she wanted to move. This was a huge risk for her. Coincidentally, Tracey ran into an older man who previously had been a neighbor of hers while growing up. He happened to mention that his daughter owned a house and was interested in renting out an apartment. When Tracey told him that she had very little money and explained her student status, he encouraged her to go by and check it out anyway. A very successful agreement was reached and Tracey still lives there today. She continues to battle the messages that say she doesn't deserve it, while at the same time pinching herself to believe it is real. Recently, she was offered a $3,000 scholarship to help her with her finances during her remaining year of school.

Jim has done a great deal of footwork around getting his finances in order. After nine months, he has found a house of his dreams and just recently put in a contract. Ann found an insect free place and moved all of her family eagerly. For the first time, she can sleep without fear. Fran presently still works as an accountant but has an excitement about her that is highly contagious. She has begun working on getting her own miniature golf course, which she plans to open in the Spring of 1993. In the meantime, she has secured an investor and is working part time at a golf course for the summer to learn more of the ins and outs of the business.

As for the visions person who wanted to be a dolphin trainer, he's now working, without experience, in such a position in Mississippi. The 40 year old woman who wants to be a pilot left Baltimore two weeks ago having been accepted in an aeronautical school in Arizona. By the way, before she left she received her private pilots license after two years of persistence and perseverance. She wants to be able to fly people to see the beauty of the Grand Canyon. Sowing, tending, reaping - with time, faith and action visions can come true.

Faith will give us the power that can overcome any negative. Faith comes to those who use it. Like the muscles in our bodies, we need to strengthen and use it often.

7

*"If God can change
a caterpillar into a butterfly,
Imagine what he can do with me."*
—Anonymous

Living in the Solution

Usually it is as a result of experiencing loss, pain, humiliation or great need, that we become ready for some kind of a Higher Power. It is at that point that a surrender occurs. We become willing to do anything as long as there is hope of things getting better. My Higher Power is called God. Yours can be anything you want it to be. Each Higher Power is personal. There is more than one. There is no scarcity of Higher Powers. They do not have to be shared. We each get to have our own who is never busy doing anything for anyone else. It is as if we have our own personal genie. In my opinion, our Higher Power is always with us; never on break or out to lunch. A Higher Power is invisible but always present. We each get to have a very special, one-to-one relationship with the Higher Power of our choice. We can lean on this Higher Power instead of trying to lean on other people. We can look for the help to come from inside, rather than outside. When we allow our minds and hearts to be still and at peace, our creative and inventive powers can be at their very best. We are then most receptive to our Higher Power. What we accept intuitively, however, may boggle the mind so it really makes no sense to try and figure everything out in our minds. Getting still means that we will not permit our fears to run us and lead us to panic. We are allowing room for something new and perhaps unknown to enter. I once heard it said, "God only visits when our mind is not at home." We need to withdraw every now and then to recharge in silence. To remain creative and inspired we need a daily spiritual renewal. It is not intellect that we need. It is inspiration and intuition. They both come from within and cannot be influenced or taken away by anything from without. It only takes an instant to be still and listen in love for divine direction in whatever we do. I don't believe that meditation needs to be long or ritualistic. What is important is that we remember we have a silent partner and it is up to us to check in for guidance and direction. With a Higher Power beside us, holding our hand, we cannot fail.

Joseph Gerzone, in his book The Shepherd says, "Even the best of us are crippled spiritually." It is his belief that we suffer from serious "spiritual malnutrition" and that people hunger for spirituality. He believes that people today are tired of packaged religion. People have not given up on God. They are simply looking in other directions. From time to time we may wonder, "how come my Higher Power doesn't give up on me?" We are partners. God needs us just as much as we need God. We are all here for one another. We each carry a piece of love that is meant in some fashion, some way to be delivered. We carry the pieces to someone else's puzzle. The answers, the hope, the resources, ideas, and clues are all sent by God through each of us to one another. As a professional I am nothing more than a messenger. I simply have to remember to get past my ego, my own agenda, and my fears so that I can do my job. When I realized who my employer really is, it occurred to me that this can all be easy. It is fun to work for God. Finding a Higher Power opens the door on the greatest adventures of life. God needs us. He's going to do everything he can to make our job possible. We only have to be creative and find many more ways of addressing it. Having abundance and sharing it, is one way. When we are prosperous, we can become a producer rather than a competitor. By being a success we can inspire others onto their own greatness. By acting with courage we can encourage others to overcome the obstacles along their pathway. Life can be very thrilling and exciting. We must be willing to step out into it with absolute faith and trust that something GOOD awaits us. Our Higher Power has promised us he will be there anytime it gets hard or scary. Whenever we call for help we will not be abandoned. We have no choice but to go forward and follow our heart. It will not rest until we do whatever it is we have been sent here to do. Our Higher Power may get a chuckle out of suggesting so many seemingly preposterous things to do. It doesn't matter. We need to put aside our will and follow wherever it is we are being led. We must trust-always trust. Keep trusting and then trust some more. Once we have surrendered and given up our plan, our will, no day will ever seem "normal" again. Fit spiritual condition means that we live life full of zest, zeal, and enthusiasm.

Getting clear on your Higher Power's purpose for you may feel difficult and unclear. What is the message that you personally have been given to deliver. To find out you must become a risk taker and know your assets. So many recovering people have done a fourth step and clearly know their defects of character . Even though the step calls for the same inventory of assets, everyone seems to struggle with this much more. We are so afraid of bragging that we never acknowledge the talents and gifts we have. We discount all that God has done, focusing only on the negative. We often overlook our beauty and the positive. Yet, we can't know our Higher Power's will for us unless we know what gifts we have to bring to the universe.

Whether you know it or not, you are truly a remarkable person. In the therapy groups I run, I encourage group members to tell this to one another. I also have individuals say to a fellow participant: "I am a truly remarkable person." This is repeated until the person listening is convinced that the person speaking really means it. Each one of us is an incredible human being; divinely appointed. The genius in you needs your permission to shine. How can we begin to do that? Take out a sheet of paper. First, write down everything that you love to do. One of you may love to garden and cook. Another may find that your greatest pleasure comes from sailing and spending time on the water. Whatever you like doing write it down. Then, write the things that you naturally do well, things that others have said you have a talent for. The third thing to put on paper is a list of the pieces of your present job (or past jobs) that you enjoy and have done success-fully. Look for the common threads that have been pointed out to you by supervisors or employers throughout all of the jobs you've ever had. Are you a good organizer? Are you good with people? Do you work well independently? The fourth list you need to make is one of your daydreams. What have you always wanted to do. In your fantasy world what feels exciting and challenging to you? What idea excites you and scares you at the same time? How can your talents and assets which you have already listed help you make your dreams come true?

To be a spiritually grounded person, we must become a risk taker. In the book <u>You Too Can Be Prosperous</u>, the author speaks of a Magic Box. It is his suggestion that you envision yourself going to this magic box anytime you want to remove whatever limitations there might be. By having the box, there would be no more poverty in any area of your life. You could go to it throughout the day, as often as you like. We each have that box. The magic box is our consciousness which is full of the ideas needed to resolve any want or need. Knowing that you can go to that box within can remove all worry, stress, and strain.

It is evident by your successes that you have gone into the magic box before. Perhaps you need to recall what some of these successes have been. Think back over the years and write down

any successes that you have had at work, in physical accomplishments, in relationships and any other area of your life. If you have
difficulty with this ask a friend. Let them help you formulate your
list. By reminding yourself of your successes, you will develop
some of the courage needed to venture forth again. Practice taking
three risks this week. If this is too hard for you, take some time to
look at all the reasons you have for not taking a risk. Give some
thought to what risk you would take today if you were guaranteed
and knew for sure that you could not fail. Then find the support
you need and do it. Let your light shine. We have whatever we
need to ensure success in any area that we decide to explore.

Whether you realize it or not, you are the light of the world.
You are a living magnet drawing people, situations, and circumstances to you according to your thoughts. The answer is not to
convince God to give you more; but rather to uncover and release
who you really are. Each of us is precious and important. Your
ability to experience good depends upon how well you understand
your worth and the value that your existence carries. Eric
Butterworth states "You owe the world a life." In turn, the
universe owes you support. Once we realize and accept this,
personal motivation, ingenuity, and opportunities will come pouring in from all directions. Good thoughts can never produce bad
results. Ideas may come as insight, intuition, imagination, and
inspiration. We need to leave the past behind and look for the very
best in every situation. Someone at a recent DA meeting admitted
that he was struggling with thinking positive . His car wasn't
running well and his scarcity thinking had him fearing the worst.
Money was tight. Finally, he felt he had no choice. The car had to
go in the shop. It no longer felt safe to drive. In a short time, he
received the dreaded phone call. You can imagine his puzzlement
when the mechanic asked him if he had squirrels where he lived.
After responding "yes," he was told that his problem was too
many peanuts in his air filter. Hoarding and stockpiling can create

problems, even when done by the squirrels. Needless to say the repair was a minor one.

We alone get to decide what kind of day (and life) we will have. We can learn to look for and expect the very best. We can begin to believe that truly wonderful things lie ahead. Wealth begins within our thoughts and feelings. As recovering people, wanting something better is an indication of our progress. It is a positive sign of our continuing growth and development. When we stay open, we will be led to pathways of new and rewarding experiences. Remember that a Higher Power never does anything to you, just for you.

In Baltimore DA, a number of people have shared with me the prosperity miracles they have realized.

- For one woman it was buying herself a diamond ring rather than telling herself she had to wait for a man.
- Another shared that new friends became her riches.
- One became self-employed after working for 13 years as a banker.
- One left a corporate position to attend the seminary.
- Another put himself through law school and graduated without debt.
- One man lost a $149,000 a year job and survived.
- A woman started a business to help elderly pack and move into nursing homes.
- Another woman joined a church and found out that once a year they give a month's collection divided up into envelopes back to the congregation.

These are just a few of the miracles. Others have included improved health, a decrease in financial fear, and entirely new level of self-esteem. There is so much for which to be thankful.

Gratitude

It is important to express gratitude. We can be grateful for ideas that enrich our lives with blessings and opportunities. We can also be grateful for the wisdom and direction we receive. We can live each day conscious of, and grateful for our health, prosperity, peace, and joy. Gratitude keeps us connected to the creative forces of the universe. Every time we express our thankfulness, we become a mental and spiritual magnet for new good. Our gratitude encourages the healing of any condition whether physical, financial or emotional. We take nothing for granted when we are in a state of gratitude. There is always something to be thankful for. As we go about counting our blessings, they will increase. By giving thanks continuously, we keep more good coming to us because our attention is on what we have, not what we don't have. Gratitude is our way of expressing a heart that is full of joy. All we need to do is stop and appreciate what is already around us. Look back at this month's prosperity. How much money has come to you so far in the form of paychecks, unemployment, interest earnings, financial gifts, refunds, coupon savings, insurance reimbursements, found money on the street, or in a coat pocket. There are numerous possibilities that may have already occurred this month. Aside from the dollars, now look at the other prosperity. What abundance have you received in love? Hugs, compliments, cards and good wishes are all enriching. Have there also been material gifts? Reflect on where you stand this month in receiving some of the good that your Higher Power has to offer. Notice how much of it was unexpected. Thank your Higher Power for all of the people and resources that have been put into your life. Begin to realize how many of your needs are now being met. Let your heart bubble over. Become a part of all that there is beautiful in the world to see. Thank your Higher Power for everything. One way to visibly do this is to actually write the words thank you on each check that you write. It doesn't matter if it is to the phone company, your landlord, or the family physician. It keeps us in tune with the services we have received. Give thanks for everything that you have and everything that you are going to receive without even knowing what that will be. Expand your thinking to include others and their needs. What you want for yourself, want for everyone. Wish health, happiness, and abundance for everyone. What we wish for others we will also wish for ourselves. Celebrate successes. There is no need to be embarrassed by the good that God has given. Look at how we can use it for spiritual purposes. Do not apologize even if you become a millionaire. Think big. Think generous. No one has to have less for you to have more. Remember with abundance there is no need for competition. As we freely give, we freely receive. Gratitude and generosity can readily go hand in hand.

Handling Success

As you begin to put some of the ideas here into practice, it is inevitable that you will begin to prosper. Within a year's time, I have seen dramatic differences in people's lives. All 12 Step Programs work. DA and it's principles are no exceptions. We can get past the negativity and limitations that we have operated out of in the past. Regardless of economic circumstances and stock market reports, we can prosper. You are apparently ready to accept this challenge. Dare to change. Dare to let go of the old ways. Dare to be rich. Good for you! You are ready to thrive, not just survive. You are already looking at the abundance you have and in connecting with your Higher Power, can be expecting even more.

There is only one remaining question; As the abundance comes in, what are we supposed to do? The first thing of course is to enjoy. Allow yourself to be happy. Don't rush around looking for a new problem. Remember to watch for all the ways that you are most likely to self-sabotage. Next, don't be afraid of change.

If anything, expect it and when it comes, be open. You can practice this by noticing your daily routines and altering them once in awhile. Take a different route to work. Go to bed an hour earlier than usual. Get an abundance of sleep for a change. Look for something new. Stay conscious and avoid going on automatic. Set a few new goals that motivate you. Look for new ideas and possibilities. Remember to stick with the lifters, and avoid the leaners. Surround yourself with the people who inspire you, the ones whom you admire the most. Constantly talk to your Higher Power. You'll need him now more than ever. There will be so many new decisions to be made. Trust. Stay focused on solutions, not the problems. You will become living proof that with God, anything is possible. Let people know your story and how you manage to become a success. Live in financial dignity. Dress prosperously. Rather than pick the cheapest item on the menu, go for what you really want. Create home and work environments that feel prosperous. Above all, don't be stingy with giving love. Our hearts have an incredible capacity to expand. Give some love to everyone you meet; even strangers. Any act of kindness will contribute to someone's day.

If you do lose what you have through self-sabotage or losing your Higher Power connection, know that your good can and will reappear. Listen for the new ideas. All the blessings that should be yours are still available. Someone once asked Henry Ford what he would do if he lost all his money and business. He stated "I would think of some other fundamental, basic need of all people, and I would supply that need more cheaply and efficiently than anyone else. In 5 years I would again be a millionaire." Persistence will pay off. Shifting from being a dreamer to a doer will work. I once heard it said that if we weren't meant to keep starting over, God wouldn't have given us Mondays. Wealth is our spiritual heritage. However, our energy does not need to go into specifically looking for money. We need to gain a clearer understanding of what our

Higher Power's will for each of us is. In doing so, we will draw good to us. In handling our success, the money itself is not what is important. It is what you do with it. The good we have, can do good. We get to decide how.

It is very important to not enable as we share. We do not want to create any emotional debts as we become more abundant. Giving gifts with no strings attached is fine. Lending money or belongings sets up an unhealthy situation. Lending can complicate and even destroy relationships. Eddy Hall suggests some guideline that may help.

1. Lend only what you can afford to give away. Give it as a gift without any expectation that it will be returned. Remove any room for possible resentment to occur. Let it go completely. Know that you have no control and are powerless once it leaves your hands.

2. If you co-sign a loan, be prepared to pay for it with the possibility of having nothing to show for the money. It is best not to co-sign for anything. It works better to give a financial gift or have that amount on hand knowing that you are obligating yourself. It is your decision. No one is forcing your signature.

3. Lend, expecting nothing in return. No favors, no rides to work, nothing is owed to you as a result of any generous gesture.

4. Make a pass-along loan. If someone won't accept a gift and wants to consider it a loan, ask them to repay by sharing that amount with someone else in need. Let them know that they don't need to tell you how or who or when they repay it. This helps those persons who are still working on receiving to have what they need. They also keep their self-esteem and integrity in tact.

5. Remember, too, that a loan can become a "secured debt" when the person in need gives you something of theirs that is equal in value as collateral for the amount they are asking to borrow.

We want to look for ways that we can help others help themselves. I adjust client fees if I know that person is open to learning about how the DA program works. Enabling people sets us up. Eventually, we feel resentful. Rescuing people leaves them feeling obligated, pitied, and damages their self-esteem. The best thing that we can give is encouragement and support. We cannot be someone's Higher Power. Each of us have our own. Let the people who come to you for help know that you believe in them and know that they can solve their problems. Then, if you want to give a gift, that's fine. But no loans. You'll destroy whatever present relationship is there.

As we are getting richer, there will be enough to share and spare. We can feel good about not hoarding. We can plan for the future without fear. There is no doubt that things will start to happen beyond your wildest dreams. When it feels like we have it all, we need to remember to:

- Give thanks;

- Believe that we deserve more;

- Live by the Golden Rule (treat yourself as well as you treat others);

- Share and give back;

- Forgive;

- Pay taxes with gratitude;

- Let go of thoughts of impending doom;

- Make God's will our will; and

- Be a power of example; inspire others.

Now that we have success, this is not a time to get even with anyone who has hurt us by not being there when we needed them. Withholding our good from others will only hurt us. More than ever, we need to look back and forgive.

Forgiveness

As we forgive, we can let go of unpleasant thoughts and details. By ridding our minds of negative thoughts, we are free to think, believe and adopt new ideas. As we forgive, we do not harbor resentments. We become more open and alert to new opportunities and blessings. We let go of any unhappiness. We begin to radiate peace. Forgiveness calls for humbly acknowledging one's own shortcomings. Forgiveness is a miracle medicine, removing the poison of hatred and bitterness. One particular client of mine had been riding in a car when it was struck by a drunk driver. This client came very close to dying and spent many months recuperating from her serious injuries. Today, her right leg remains held together by pins and wires and a long iron rod beneath her skin. Great anger and bitterness followed long after her physical pain had begun to subside. Family members and even her doctor could not convince her to let go of the ill will she harbored towards this person. However, one evening, many months later, as she watched the news she saw a young woman in a wheelchair, paralyzed from her waist down, by a similar accident. When my client saw this she began to cry and cry. When asked what was wrong, she said that she realized the person on TV could have been her. At that point in time, this client became aware of what pain her anger and resentment was causing her. By now she had ulcers and many other physical symptoms. Experiencing an enormous gratitude towards being alive helped her get beyond the hatred she had for another's self-will and irresponsible behavior which had so profoundly affected her.

Forgiveness is a decision. Without forgiveness there is anger, resentment, and sometimes guilt over the way we feel. When we hold onto hurt, we cannot love. As we wall off that person, we shut out others, too. We need to remember that forgiveness frees the forgiver. Forgiveness is:

* Accepting a person as he is and allowing him to have shortcomings;
* Not taking everything personally;
* Accepting someone's apology;
* Letting an incident go;
* Being willing to forget;
* Not being stubborn, self-righteous or proud; and
* Admitting we are powerless over people, places and things.

When we are willing to let go of resentment, there is new power released. We can feel whole again. Yet, some hurts feel too great to forgive. At those times it helps to think of the greatest wrong you have ever done and how much you wanted to be forgiven. Give that gift to someone else. Pray for the courage and willingness to say, "I'm sorry." We are human and it is foolish to think that we will never make a mistake. Saying you're sorry is a simple way of acknowledging that we have shortcomings and that every now and then they will get in the way.

Forgiving our debtors is crucial to having more prosperity in our lives. When we can't let go of what someone owes us, we become resentful and stay focused on the debt. Over time this will lead us to making that person our Higher Power and living in financial fear. One person's debt to us cannot keep us from our good. There are many avenues good will comes to us. So that I personally don't fall into the trap of having a person become my Higher Power, I have developed a debt forgiveness letter. I mailed one to someone who damaged my car in an accident and having no insurance, refused to pay. On occasion, when I know I'm not enabling, I will also send a letter to a client who is without funds over a long period of time. In my debt forgiveness letter I ask only that the person receiving the letter in turn forgive someone who is indebted to them. By sending these letters, I am then free to move on. I stop trying to force something to happen and I no longer make myself crazy in the process. I can then get on with receiving the good my Higher Power has intended for me. Sometimes just having a sense of humor about things can help.

Humor

We are all born with a sense of humor. Developing it is essential to our spirituality. Dr. Joel Goodman, publisher of "Laughing Matters" doesn't believe it was any accident that the Great Depression of the 1930's happened when Jack Benny, Bob Hope, Burns and Allen, Laurel and Hardy, and the Marx Brothers all became so popular. For most of us, there has been no real cultivation or encouragement of our sense of humor. For me it takes practice. I have to look for humor. I now make it a point to buy funny books. I spend hours trying to create up funny answering machine messages. I rent humorous movies. With Dr. Goodman's help, I have learned to watch for humor in print. He encourages people to swap humor and ideas. Writing funny sayings in your checkbook for example, allows you to laugh all the way to the bank. Making up funny definitions stimulates our creative juices. For example, "A procrastinator is a person who has hardening of the oughteries." A good starting point is to notice signs such as the one outside a church in Atlanta that said, "We will not be undersouled!" Others that have tickled my funny bone include a sign seen on the door of a psychiatric ward which states, "Please do not disturb further." By identifying someone whose humor you admire, it becomes a lot easier to address life's everyday problems. Anytime I'm up against a tough situation, I try to remember to ask myself: How would Bill Cosby handle this one. I may just discover a little of him in me yet. Laughter and feelings of happiness need to be developed in ways that we form other habits. Life can be ordinary or it can be great. We do not need to wait for happiness. We can practice being enthusiastic and light about all of life. A smile can brighten anyone's day. A smile can reflect peace, joy, and love. It actually takes less muscles to smile then it does to frown. Smiles are also contagious. Give yourself a face lift. It may be a simple smile that helps someone else climb whatever hill it is they may have to climb. As a man named Ed Smith once remarked, "When you help someone up a hill, you're that much nearer the top yourself." Feeling joyous won't be automatic. Initially, we may need to look for and identify the times when we have that feeling. Just like in the beginning of recovery, we had to label the times when we were sad or angry, we will need to identify the feeling of joy and bring it to our own awareness. We are joyous when we are alert, awake, and feel glad to be alive. No one has the power to take away our joy unless we let them. Joy comes from within. By exploring life, we can become excited in healthy, happy ways. To experience joy, we must be able to return to our child-like self and see the world through the eyes of a discoverer; thrilled with each and every new treasure. We live life with enthusiasm. Try just for a day to do everything with zeal. When you take a walk, consciously choose to do it with zest and see how it feels. Do your dishes or make your bed in the same manner, but with enthusiasm. Chances are, you may find yourself unexpectedly joyous and energized. The greatest way to appreciate life is to live with passion, wonder, and joy.

As a wise woman, Betty Garrett once said, "...years may wrinkle the skin, but living without enthusiasm will wrinkle the soul."

If you really can't handle having things be good, go back to negative thinking. Begin to think only about yourself. Focus on the past. Review every mistake you ever made. Remind yourself of every time someone treated you unkindly. Think about your body. Look for some ache or pain to focus on. Imagine that it is cancer and that you are going to die. Think about your age, telling yourself that you are going downhill fast. Dwell on all the problems that exist on your job, do this especially on the weekend. I am sure that before very long, with this kind of thinking, you will be quite successful in eliminating any possibility of joy. Hopefully, by now you won't want to return to the misery that can be found there.

So perhaps you are ready to be happy, joyous, and free. If so, may all your dreams come true. It has been two years since I had a vision of writing this book. Seeing it completed, assures me once again, if I believe, that Miracles Do Happen! I leave you with one final message - the Twenty Third Psalm revised. May it carry you far.

A Prosperity Treatment

The Lord is my banker; my credit is good.

He maketh me to lie down in the consciousness of
 omnipresent abundance;

 He giveth me the key to His strongbox.

He restoreth my faith in His riches;

He guideth me in the paths of prosperity for His name's sake.

Yea, though I walk in the very shadow of debt, I shall fear
 no evil, for Thou art with me;

Thy silver and Thy gold, they secure me.

Thou preparest a way for me in the presence of the collector;

Thou fillest my wallet with plenty: my measure runneth over.
Surely goodness and plenty will follow me all the days
   of my life.
And I shall do business in the name of the Lord forever.

—Anonymous

PROMISES as reprinted from Alcoholics
Anonymous, pp. 83-84 with permission of
AA World Services.*

If we are painstaking about this phase of our development,
we will be amazed before we are half way through. **We are going
to know** a new freedom and a new happiness. **We will not regret**
the past nor wish to shut the door on it. **We will comprehend** the
word serenity and we will know peace. **No matter** how far down
the scale we have gone, we will see how our experience can
benefit others. **That feeling** of uselessness and self-pity will
disappear. **We will lose** interest in selfish things and gain interest
in our fellows. **Self-seeking** will slip away. **Our whole attitude
and outlook** upon life will change. **Fear of people** and economic
insecurity will leave us. **We will intuitively know** how to handle
situations that used to baffle us. **We suddenly realize** that God is
doing for us what we could not do for ourselves.

Are these extravagant promises? We think not. They are
being fulfilled among us – sometimes quickly, sometimes slowly.
They will always materialize if we work for them.

Bibliography

Berg, Adriane. *How to Stop Fighting About Money and Make Some.* New York: Avon Books.

Butterworth, Eric. *Spiritual Economics: The Prosperity Process.*

Caddy, Eileen. *Opening Doors Within.* Foves, Scotland: The Findhorn Press.

Collins, Vincent. *Partnership.* St. Meinrad, Indiana: Abbey Press Publications, 1962.

Frank, Amalie. *Consciousness Building Group Handbook to Prosperity.* Washington, D.C.: Sun Search, Inc.

Girzone, Joseph F. *Joshua The Shepherd.* New York, New York: Macmillan Publishing Co.

Goodwin, Matthew Oliver. *Numerology: The Complete Guide. Vol. 1: The Personality Reading.* North Hollywood, California: Newcastle Publishing Co., Inc., 1981.

Gordon, Arthur. *A Touch of Wonder.* New York, New York: The Berkley Publishing Group.

Hurnard, Hannah. *Hinds' Feet on High Places.* Wheaton, Illinois: Tyndale House Publisher, Inc.

Lanphear, Roger. *Money Making.* San Diego, California: Unified Publications.

"Laughing Matters" Joel Goodman, editor, Volume 8: No.3, Saratoga Springs, New York.

Laut, Phil. *Money is My Friend.* Trinity Publications.

Mandino, Og. *Greatest Miracle in the World.* New York: Bantam Books.

Mundis, Jerrold. *How to Get Out of Debt, Stay Out of Debt and Live Prosperously.* Bantam Books.

Murphy, Joseph. *Your Infinite Power to be Rich.* West Nyack, New York: Parker Publishing Company.

Perkins-Reed, Marcia. *When 9 to 5 Isn't Enough.* Santa Monica, California: Hay House, Inc.

Ponder, Catherine. *Open Your Mind to Prosperity.* Marina del Rey, California: DeVorss and Company.

Ponder, Catherine. *The Millionaires of Genesis: Their Prosperity Secrets for You.*

Robinson, Bryan. *Work Addiction.* Deerfield Beach Florida: Health Communications.

Ross, Ph.D., Ruth. *Prospering Woman: A Complete Guide to Achieving the Full, Abundant Life.* New York: Bantam Books.

Russell, Robert. *You, too, Can Be Prosperous: Studies in Prosperity.* DeVorss Publications.

Shames, Lawrence. *The Hunger For More.* New York, New York: Times Book

Speller, Dr. Jon. *Seed Money in Action.* New York, New York: Morning Star Press.

Stoddard, Alexandra. *Daring to Be Yourself.* New York, New York: Doubleday.

Thomas, Arthur G. *Abundance is Your Right.* Redondo Beach, California: Los Arboles Publications.

Thomas, Carl. *The Heart Knows.* Lake Dallas, Texas: Love Notes Press.

"Getting the Most Out of Life" *Reader's Digest.* July 1991, p.17.

"The Forbes Four Hundred" *Forbes Magazine.* October 22, 1990, Vol. 146, No. 9.

"The List of Billionaires" *Fortune Magazine.* September 10, 1990, Vol. 122, No. 6.

"The World's Billionaires" *Forbes Magazine.* July 23, 1990, Vol. 145, No. 2.

General Service Board of DA, P.O. Box 400 Grand Central Station New York, NY 10163-0400 (212)-969-0710. There are over 425 Debtors Anonymous groups in 37 of the United States and five foreign countries. Telephone numbers of Debtors Anonymous Intergroups in a few other cities include:

Northern California 415-457-3835

Southern California 213-271-3002

Washington DC, Virginia 703-284-2102

Maryland 410-825-7455

Atlanta DA Intergroup 404-436-6638,
P.O. Box 13158 Atlanta Da Intergroup

Dallas DA Intergroup 214-504-6332
Dale Pynes 2022 Palo Alto Dr.
Carrollton, TX 75006

New England Intergroup 617-642-1913
P.O. Box 390412 Cambridge, Ma.